"Get the hell off this ship!"

"Get the hell off this ship!"
Memoir of a USS *Liscome Bay* Survivor in World War II

JAMES CLAUDE BEASLEY

Edited by ELSIE L. BEASLEY

McFarland & Company, Inc., Publishers
Jefferson, North Carolina

LIBRARY OF CONGRESS CATALOGUING-IN-PUBLICATION DATA

Names: Beasley, James Claude, 1924– author. | Beasley, Elsie L., editor.
Title: "Get the hell off this ship!" : memoir of a USS Liscome Bay survivor in World War II / James Claude Beasley ; edited by Elsie L. Beasley.
Other titles: Memoir of a USS Liscome Bay survivor in World War II
Description: Jefferson, North Carolina : McFarland & Company, Inc., Publishers, [2018] | Includes bibliographical references and index.
Identifiers: LCCN 2018004776 | ISBN 9781476673288 (softcover : acid free paper) ∞
Subjects: LCSH: Beasley, James Claude, 1924– | Liscome Bay (Escort Carrier : CVE 56) | World War, 1939–1945—Naval operations, American. | World War, 1939–1945—Campaigns—Kiribati. | World War, 1939–1945—Campaigns—Pacific Area.
Classification: LCC D774.L57 B43 2018 | DDC 940.54/5973092 [B] —dc23
LC record available at https://lccn.loc.gov/2018004776

BRITISH LIBRARY CATALOGUING DATA ARE AVAILABLE

ISBN (print) 978-1-4766-7328-8
ISBN (ebook) 978-1-4766-3236-0

© 2018 Elsie L. Beasley. All rights reserved

No part of this book may be reproduced or transmitted in any form or by any means, electronic or mechanical, including photocopying or recording, or by any information storage and retrieval system, without permission in writing from the publisher.

Front cover: James Claude Beasley official Navy photograph; medals earned in Navy battles in World War II

Printed in the United States of America

McFarland & Company, Inc., Publishers
 Box 611, Jefferson, North Carolina 28640
  www.mcfarlandpub.com

To my wife, Elsie, who listened to my stories over and over. There were many years I did not discuss my experiences in the Navy with anyone. After I finally began to tell about them, she encouraged me to make a written record. Elsie wanted the children to know what I had encountered and my reactions. I think I did not speak of those years hoping I would forget most of the bad events, but that was not to be.

To my children who heard only bits and pieces of my years of service in the Navy during World War II but seemed to understand that the war helped to shape my whole life.

To my grandchildren who seem in awe of what life was like for me as a teenager in time of war and how I managed to survive!

Thanks to Marilyn Ball who was invaluable in helping with the photographs and illustrations.

—James Claude Beasley (1928–2011)

Table of Contents

Preface   1

1. Early Life at Home   3
2. School Days   6
3. A New Life   11
4. Training for War   15
5. Practicing for Battle   21
6. Hawaii   26
7. Fun and Fight   30
8. Calm Before the Storm   35
9. Tragedy   38
10. Survival   44
11. Rescued   47
12. Return to Hawaii   52
13. In the Hospital   56
14. Recovery   61
15. Home for Christmas   66
16. Guam   71
17. Leyte Island   76
18. Second Battle of Leyte   81
19. Luzon   84
20. Time for Reflection   88
21. Okinawa   93

Table of Contents

22.	In Seattle	97
23.	The Surprise	103
24.	The Bomb	106
25.	War Is Over	109
26.	Discharge and Transition	114
27.	Back Home	117
28.	Navy Friends	121
29.	We Meet Again	127
30.	Remembering	143
31.	The Grand Finale	148

Epilogue	152
Bibliography	157
Index	159

Preface

This book is not intended to be the full story of my life, but rather an account of the time I spent in the Navy during World War II. However, I will begin with several stories of my early life as I recall the events, to help explain my background before entering the Navy. It will also aid in understanding the feelings and emotions I felt as a young man away from home in a totally new environment.

I, like most other teenagers who began serving in the military, found myself in many unusual and challenging situations. I could not imagine the true horrors of war and the sadness it brought. It was a real adventure! From the day I enlisted with great anticipation, excitement, and some uncertainty, to the day I received my honorable discharge, I was totally dedicated to the Navy and the job I was expected to perform.

Remembering all these experiences brings to mind great joy and happiness as well as sadness and sorrow. The wonderful and lasting friendships I made over a period of almost four years will always be with me. The great places I visited still impress me and have added much to my life. However, there is another side I remember too, the dark side. Those times linger and are very disturbing. I recall how we learned to live with danger day and night. At times, I think I can hear the sounds of pain and hurting among my buddies. The worst part is thinking of the many good friends that never made it home to live out their dreams. I was wonderfully blessed! I was forced to grow up in a hurry. I can hardly believe that I began this important part of my life when I was only eighteen!

1

Early Life at Home

In 1924 in Stokes County, North Carolina, a baby boy was born to Maggie Lawson and James Arthur Beasley. This healthy boy arrived November 25, kicking, screaming and crying! He was given the name James Claude Beasley. I really don't remember this important event because that baby was me.

When I was sixteen months old I got a baby brother, another event I do not remember. However, two years later I got a second baby brother, an event I well remember! I knew at a very early age I was blessed with a good memory and took advantage of the talent.

One morning there was much excitement around the house. The family doctor drove up our driveway in his new black Ford car. He quickly jumped out carrying his well-worn medicine bag and rushed into the house. Soon Daddy walked into the living room and came over to me (now more than three years old), as I played with my two-year-old brother, Clarence. Daddy suggested we go with him down the road to the country store and get some candy. We jumped up! Who would turn down an invitation like that?

While holding hands with Daddy, we hopped and skipped along the side of the road. When a car came by we moved over into the grass to let it pass. It seemed a long way to the store—and the candy!

When we entered the store, a very nice man greeted us. He and Daddy talked while my brother and I looked at all the jars of candy. The shelf was filled with big jars of different colors, shapes, and sizes of candy. Daddy told us that we could each pick out two pieces. That was a hard job! Should I choose the biggest or the brightest? When we had made our choices and were ready to eat a piece of the candy, the nice man handed Clarence and me each a big piece of sweet chocolate as a gift. We gladly accepted and quickly put his gift in our mouths. It was so good! What a nice man! But why was he giving us a gift?

We were the happiest little boys. We talked, played and ate candy all the way home. Just as I entered the yard, I heard a baby cry and saw the doctor getting into his car to leave. Our neighbor, a friend of my mother, was on the porch smiling.

She greeted us with "You boys have a healthy baby brother!" That was the beginning of my cherished memories.

We were a happy family, Mama, Daddy, and three little boys. We were buying a house. Daddy had a good job at the furniture factory. Mama stayed busy at home. We played all day without a care in the world. One day something strange happened that I did not understand. Paul, Clarence and I were playing in the yard when Daddy came home early from work. I was curious because I never knew him to leave his job until late in the afternoon, about suppertime. Unseen, I slipped into the house. Daddy was sitting at the kitchen table with his head in his hands and he was crying. Mama was standing beside him with her hand on his shoulder. I was very quiet and listened to what was being said.

James Claude Beasley, 1928.

"I don't know what we are going to do. I have been laid off at the factory. I have no job," Daddy said with much sadness in his voice. Trying to console him, Mama said, "I'm sure it is only temporary. They will probably call you back in a few days."

Daddy went on to explain, "I'm not the only one; all my friends and fellow workers were told it would be for a long time and not to plan on coming back. If, or when, we were needed they would get in touch with us." He continued, "It's the depression. It is hitting the furniture business hard. No one is able to buy what we make, so the factory is closing its entire operation."

That was in 1929 and I was five years old. I thought, "A depression? What is a depression?" I soon learned the full meaning of the word and the situation we were in. Daddy could only find odd jobs. He might work a few hours for a friend who was able to pay very little or maybe nothing at all. Handyman

1. Early Life at Home

jobs were few and far between. Daddy tried hard to keep up our house payments but was unsuccessful. We lost our home!

I soon learned we were among the fortunate families in the area. Mama's parents lived on a farm out in the country and when her father died her mother continued to live there. In addition to her house, my grandmother had a vacant house on the land just across the hill from hers. It was small and in need of repairs but it was a place to call home. As a widow, she was anxious for us to occupy a house near her. She offered it to Mama and Daddy for free! We were happy to accept her offer.

The farm was a great place for boys. Why did we need money? We had everything anyone could want. There was an orchard with all kinds of fruit trees—apples, pears and plums—as well as several grapevines. We had a big potato patch and vegetables of every description in the garden. There were large and small trees we cut for firewood to keep us warm and cook our food. We had chickens for meat and eggs. There were rabbits and squirrels in the wooded area. Our survival needs were met but the best part was the fun we had! We climbed trees, waded in the creek, made a swing with the grapevine. But best of all, Daddy had time to take us fishing. How proud we were to bring fish home for supper!

2

School Days

When I turned six, I thought I was almost a grown man. I could do lots of inside and outside chores. I became rather independent and did not need—or want—anyone to help me. "I can do it myself!" I told everyone who tried to assist me.

My grandmother, Martha Lawson, called me aside one day with a request. "Would you come over to my house and live with me?" Then she added, "You could stay with me at night and help with the chores around the house during the day. I would like to have your company." I was simply delighted! I knew I would miss my family, but they were only a short distance away, just across the hill. My answer was an emphatic "Yes!"

I packed my meager belongings in a paper sack and over the hill I went to Grandmother's house. She explained what my chores would be: bring in the firewood for the fireplace and the cook stove, feed the dog named Dice (it was white with black spots), feed the chickens and gather eggs, pick fruits and herbs at her request, trap and skin rabbits to cook, and keep her company. What a life that would be!

I became the man of the house, doing things I liked to do while helping Grandmother, too. In return, she taught me songs, read to me and made fried apple pies on the coals in the fireplace. If I did extra jobs she paid me a nickel when the task was finished. (I still have the first nickel I earned.) She taught me about the natural world as we took walks. We were very happy together.

When I started school, I was still living with my grandmother. One evening after supper, about a week before I was to enter first grade, she told me she had a surprise for me. A surprise? What could it be? She handed me the prettiest sweater I had ever seen. Of course I had to try it on. I remembered seeing her knitting whenever she had some spare time but I never asked what she was making. After I had worn the sweater awhile she said I should take it off and save it for my first day of school.

"I have another gift for you," she said as she brought out a small package.

2. School Days

I jumped up and down and laughed with joy when she presented me with a cap—not just a cap, but a cap with aviator's goggles attached to it! I knew I was the luckiest boy alive.

My days in first grade were happy times. Daddy walked the mile to and from school with me the first week. He walked but he let me ride our mule. The second week I was allowed to ride the big yellow school bus with children of all ages. I liked my teacher and made lots of friends. At the end of the long day, I looked forward to getting back home to a glass of cold milk and one of grandmother's fried apple pies.

I saw some of my family every day and now I had a baby sister, Ruby. All was going so well for me when an unex-

Grandfather John Beasley.

pected tragedy struck. Grandmother had a fatal heart attack! I could not comprehend what might come next. What was I to do? My world that was so perfect had ended. I could not imagine her being gone. I would miss her and the good life we shared. There would be no more evenings of study, reading and talking—and no more fried apple pies after school each day. The one thing I knew was that days with my grandmother would be treasured for the rest of my life.

About every two or three weeks on Saturday morning, when weather permitted, Grandmother and I would take a walk in the woods, looking for special herbs. She showed me what to gather. Sometimes she would tell me to pick certain leaves or twigs from a bush. She showed me which roots to dig and how to take bark from some special tree. She put everything in a woven basket and carried our findings home. After each plant was prepared separately, everything was mixed together. The dark liquid was stored in a glass jar, carefully handled and stored in her flour cabinet. Every morning before breakfast she would pour a small amount into a cup and drink it. She told me her "bitters" kept her healthy. When she died, I thought, "Grandmother, you should have been drinking more of your bitters." Many times I have wished I had learned about her herbs and how she prepared them.

I moved back home with my parents and siblings and adjusted without any problems. After a year or two on the farm, Daddy got his old job back at the furniture factory. Things were getting better for us and our friends. We rented a house in Mt. Airy and moved into town nearer Daddy's work. I couldn't forget the good times on the farm with my grandmother but I made new friends and found new activities in which to participate. I attended an elementary school nearby and walked with neighbors to school. I became more aware of my good memory as the years passed because I was not fond of homework but was very attentive in class so I did all right grade-wise.

James Claude Beasley high school graduation.

When I was nine years old, I began working for money. I helped relatives with farm work and neighbors with their yards. The family continued to grow in number. Even a nickel or dime now and then seemed important to the family.

When I was old enough to qualify, I took a paper route and thought I was going to get rich when I saved enough money to buy a bicycle! I swept the floors and ran errands for my grandfather John Beasley at the small country store he owned. He was also a Free Will Baptist preacher. Sometimes I pondered about the promises he made me. There were days I was in need of a little money but at the end of the work day he would say, "I'll pay you tomorrow." Frequently, tomorrow never came.

2. School Days

When I was in high school I was very serious about having a job to earn money to help support my family, but especially for all my own expenses. There were now seven children and we were always in need of something. I worked after school and on weekends when school was in session. During the summer I worked the full four months of vacation time. My employers told me I was a dedicated worker so I never failed to find a good-paying job—a good-paying job for the late 1930s, that is. I was interested in playing on the school's sports teams and knew my parents could not afford to help me pay for equipment and travel. After buying my clothes and other general necessities, I purchased my sports supplies. Somehow I usually saved enough money for a Saturday night movie and a bag of popcorn.

Speaking of sports—baseball was always my favorite and I played on the school team all four years of high school. On Sunday afternoons I was among a group of teenagers who gathered on the field for a pick-up baseball game. I remember one neighborhood boy in particular who came to play most Sundays. He did not go to our high school but we welcomed him. He was likeable and very agreeable but not a star player. Most of the boys who showed up to play were like me, financially limited, and we never knew if we would have balls, bats and gloves to even play baseball. However, we knew when this boy came we could count on having a fun afternoon. He came with all the paraphernalia needed and shared with any and all of us. His name was Andy Griffith! We enjoyed his company but had no idea how well known and popular he would become.

I was seventeen, a senior in high school and living at home on December 7, 1941. How well I remember the shock of the surprise bombing of Pearl Harbor by the Japanese! I had been making my own decisions and earning my way for several years, but now what? This event changed my whole way of thinking about my future plans.

Several of my teachers were suggesting college and helping me make plans to attend. I liked the idea! My grades were not great but acceptable and I was considered a good all-around student. Elon College had offered to help me financially and I was considering other scholarships also.

I graduated from Franklin High School in May of 1942. I spent the summer working and thinking. I worked at a dairy making ice cream. I worked in the dye room of a sock knitting mill. In my extra time I helped on tobacco farms. I knew I did not want to do either of those jobs for the rest of my life! Should I go to college? Many of my friends were enlisting in the military and I knew in November I would be eligible for the draft. The war situation wors-

"Get the hell off this ship!"

ened and I had to make an important decision. I could not envision myself in the Army so I decided to join the Navy. College would have to wait.

The war news went from bad to worse and in my mind I knew what I had to do. My family was against the idea of me enlisting so I had to get help from a friend of Daddy's. He convinced my parents that it would be better for me to choose the branch of service I preferred rather than be drafted into the Army. Still rather reluctantly, Daddy signed my enlistment papers in the Navy recruiter's office in Mt. Airy. I was going into the Navy to see the world!

3

A New Life

On November 25, 1942, I became eighteen years old. The war news was becoming increasingly disturbing. There were more and more hard battles being fought in Europe and in the Pacific area. The number of casualties continued to grow rapidly as the Allied Forces lost ground on all fronts.

I had made up my mind to enlist in the Navy. On December 15, 1942, in Winston-Salem, I officially became a member of the United States Navy. There I boarded a bus with other enlistees from the area and I headed for Raleigh. As soon as we arrived we were directed to line up for numerous examinations. I knew I was a sailor when the physical examination and all the other tests were completed. What a day! I was well aware that was only the beginning and the easy part. There would be much more to come in the future.

The first commanding order was given to me along with my serial number. An officer in a very firm voice told me, "You memorize this number and keep it a secret from everybody!" I was thankful for my good memory; after one look at the number I knew it and never forgot it. I felt very proud to have been so quickly accepted into the Navy and was most pleased to have made that choice for myself. There were many sad young men that day who were turned away because they did not meet the strict requirements. After spending one night in a make-shift barracks in Raleigh, we were loaded onto a train headed for Illinois. While traveling I recalled studying maps of the United States in school and I tried to visualize where we were going. I was excited about my new adventure!

At the beginning of the train trip, we all talked and became acquainted with each other. There was mostly light-hearted conversation—where in North Carolina we were from, the schools we attended and the family we left behind. Sometimes we spoke of what the future might hold, but of course none of us thought it would be anything other than great!

As we continued to ride hour after hour, we talked less and thought

"Get the hell off this ship!"

Graduation, Great Lakes Naval Training Station. James Beasley second row, fourth from left.

more. My thoughts seemed to go in the direction of uncertainty. I said to myself, "Right now I am going to the Great Lakes Naval Training Station…" but I could not finish the sentence. I had no idea what was to follow. I was at the mercy of my superiors and eventually maybe at the mercy of my enemies. Though I felt a little confused as to my future, I was totally satisfied with my decision. All will go well!

Any concerns I had were short-lived and as the trip progressed I felt excitement as I looked at the pretty country through which we were passing. Some of the towns resembled Mt. Airy. I enjoyed the stops for food and drinks. Soon before us was the big city of Chicago! What a city! I had never seen anything like that back home. Most of the other boys were also amazed at the sight we were witnessing.

On December 17, 1942, I began my Navy training program as an apprentice seaman in one of the coldest spots on the face of the earth—so I thought—the Great Lakes Naval Training Station! The cold and the constant wind in dead of winter was a challenge to contend with during the months I trained there. Actually, it was a very pretty place. The base was a large training facility located on Lake Michigan and was lively and busy all the time. We did not have much free time to explore with our full schedule. The officers and instructors kept us occupied training and studying.

The Navy had its own photographic studio and made a picture of each sailor to send home to family. I was proud to be seen in my uniform and happy to be able to show how good I looked in my new uniform. The family

3. A New Life

was pleased to have my photo sitting in plain view to show to all who came for a visit. My brothers, Clarence and Paul, were impressed to see their big brother in his new dress outfit. Both joined the Navy when they came of age.

For the first three months of training my life consisted of being stuck with needles, marching on the icy ground, preparing for daily inspection, doing what I was commanded to do, eating and sleeping when and where I was told. I'll always remember when my head was shaved and I went around bald in minus zero temperatures! My head was so cold I could hardly think. It seemed the hair would never grow back, but it did, only to be cut again. Thank goodness for the sailor's cap. When I least expected it, some officer would ask for my serial number and I had no trouble calling out quickly, "657–34–69."

At times I was so exhausted I could hardly think, but most nights I would lie in my bunk pondering many things. I was in a room with about fifteen other young men who probably thought about the same things. Family, home, friends, the present and the future were topics I knew we all had in mind, and even talked about. We were training for war—and what would come next? That was a serious question none of us could answer. As a typical little boy at home, in school and playing with friends, I never dreamed of being involved in a situation like I was experiencing, and I kept thinking, "I am only eighteen!" The idea would not leave me.

I survived Great Lakes boot camp without freezing to death from the cold winds and snow coming off of Lake Michigan. I did have several mishaps. I had a bad bout with the flu which turned into pneumonia and I ended up in the hospital. I was scheduled to be given my discharge from the hospital on graduation day. It was a terribly cold day and the ground was covered with ice. For some reason there was a delay of several hours in my discharge and I was about to miss the ceremony. No way would I let that happen!

I ran to the barracks, put on my white dress uniform and ran across the icy ground to the location of the ceremony. My feet slid out from under me. When I fell I cut my knee open, got blood on my clean white uniform and ended up back in the hospital! It was a sad situation. All my new friends graduated and shipped out to their next assignment, and I lay in a hospital bed in Great Lakes Naval Training Station!

I was placed with another group and in about two weeks I graduated from boot camp, so I would be going on, but the feeling of pride had left me. I had no one to celebrate with because I had not trained with these persons. I did not even know their names.

"Get the hell off this ship!"

When I completed boot camp I had the rank of Seaman 2c and like most sailors I was very proud to show off my uniform and rank. I had learned that girls were proud to be seen with a young man in his dress uniform. In fact, it seemed the ladies thought all sailors were very handsome.

I had been in boot camp for three months and I was ready for the next phase of training. On March 19, 1943, I left on a train headed west and arrived at Farragut, Idaho. I had time to reminisce while getting to my new destination. A lot had happened to me in the last few months and I knew I was growing up in a hurry. I was very excited and pleased with my decision to enlist in the U.S. Navy. It was difficult to believe I was still only eighteen!

4

Training for War

At the Great Lakes Naval Training Station we were taught to be "military minded." All forms of discipline were stressed in everything we did. First and foremost was the necessity for physical fitness for performance and endurance. We were drilled daily in the discipline of listening and following orders. We were instructed on the importance of "no lose talk, remain silent on military matters." We were mentally challenged for a quick and accurate response. Our conduct and patterns of behavior were constantly judged by our superiors. Any one of these actions might someday determine whether we lived or died. Those were serious thoughts for a young man. Later, I realized the value and importance of the firm training.

Paul Brown was one of my instructors at Great Lakes. He was a coach of the Cleveland football team and was such an outstanding coach the team was named for him—the Cleveland Browns. I could understand the reason for his popularity. He believed in being tough, but in a helpful and constructive way. I consider him the best instructor I had while in the Navy. All the men admired his method of teaching and directing those under his command.

We were still unprepared to get involved in battle. We had to specialize in a particular field. We needed to choose for our training a field we could excel in. I was happy to have scored in the top 10 percent of the class. This enabled me to choose the kind of training I preferred. I chose to go to signal school thus I ended up in Idaho.

The value of communication cannot be overstated and its importance in time of war was impressed on all of us who went into the signal corps. My four-month-long training course at the Farragut Naval Training Station was intense and challenging. We were drilled in Morse code. It was used to send and receive messages by wire and also by lights. One error could cause catastrophic consequences. Flag position, or semaphore, was another way of giving signals or sending messages. I studied diligently and my good memory served me well. With practice I became a very good signalman. Many of my classmates found the course too difficult and transferred to another field of training.

There were other military bases where signal school training was offered, but I believe I was in the best location and at the choice school. Farragut was one of the world's largest naval bases. It was named for the famous Civil War admiral David Glasgow Farragut. There were more than seven hundred and fifty buildings. The hospital alone had seven miles of corridors. In the base's brief four-year history, 1942–1946, it served more than 300,000 men like me as a rite of passage. In the last years, it served as a prisoner of war camp for German soldiers. The base has become a part of Farragut State Park, with a museum dedicated to its operation in World War II. I went back for a visit in May 1992 (49 years after being stationed there) and found things quite different but still impressive. I was fortunate to have been assigned to Farragut!

James Beasley in Navy signal school at Farragut, Idaho.

While in Idaho, I made a special effort to visit some of the surrounding countryside and nearby towns. The beautiful town of Coeur d'Alene was not far from our base. I really enjoyed visiting there from time to time. I thought Lake Coeur d'Alene was the most beautiful lake I had ever seen! Its shimmering ripples sparkled in the sunlight and the water was crystal clear.

I wrote home several times telling Daddy about the great fishing streams in the area where I was stationed. The cold, fast-moving water flowing through the valleys reminded me of the mountain streams in North Carolina. I never had a chance to try fishing but told Daddy sometime in the future I wished he and I could visit Idaho and fish together.

4. Training for War

After four months of signalman school, I completed the course and was promoted to the rank of Seaman 1st class. I received my assignment and went by train to Bremerton, Washington, on July 20, 1943. A fellow signalman and I arrived at our supposed destination to take our gear on our ship at the Bremerton Dock. The whole area was covered with naval personnel. There were more ships in the Puget Sound than fish!

We stood amazed at the sights before us when a change in our orders was given. The complete crew of our ship was stranded at the dock! Our ship was not ready for us to board and with the changes it might not be completed for months. That did not sit well with our anxious and experienced captain. He sprung into action! We were lodged and waited to see what would happen next. We were not informed as to what was being done or how things were progressing, but on July 30, 1943, we received orders for all crew members to gather at the Puget Sound Naval Yard with our belongings. Carrying our heavy sea bags we marched on to a ferry headed for Seattle, which was just across the sound. In Seattle, we boarded a train and rode all night to Astoria, Oregon. The captain had found us a ship named *Liscome Bay*. Finally we would be on our way to somewhere in the Pacific. When we would leave and where we would go was unknown. Only time would tell.

The *Liscome Bay* was a small aircraft carrier that had been launched in

Signal school graduation at Farragut, Idaho. James Beasley third row, at right.

"Get the hell off this ship!"

Vancouver, Washington, at the Kaiser shipyards. It had traveled down the Columbia River to Astoria for her final fittings. After all our crew arrived, the ship was checked over carefully. Some mechanical problems were discovered and we could not board her. Now what? Luck did not seem to be with us.

With our sea bags still packed, the crew was taken to a Navy facility nearby. We were in a very nice camp for about a week. It was called Camp Cladstrop and was located where Lewis and Clark spent the winter in their western exploration. We slept in wooden buildings, had good food served in a nice dining area and had lots of free time. For recreation, we visited the beach resort of Seaside, walked along the Columbia River, played baseball and slept. Not a bad situation but all of us were ready to get on with the job we were prepared to do.

Our life of leisure ended on Saturday morning, August 7, 1943, when we were called to formation. At this time there were about six hundred crew members anxiously preparing to board ship, our new home. Most of the crew were young and green—like me—but the officers were well trained and had

The *Liscome Bay* at the Navy dock in Astoria, Oregon (Navy Archives).

4. Training for War

The *Liscome Bay*'s commissioning ceremony, August 7, 1943. Left to right: Captain Irving D. Wiltsie, Commander Finley E. Hall, and an unidentified official (Navy Archives).

previous experiences in the Navy. Although we came from many regions of the United States with various backgrounds, we were together—we were one!

We found our quarters, unpacked, put on dress uniforms and gathered on the flight deck. The *Liscome Bay* was formally commissioned as a part of the Pacific fleet of the United States of America! I proudly stood on the ship's bridge at my signal station while watching the ceremony. Impressive! I felt a devotion and loyalty to the Navy I had not felt before. The *Liscome Bay* was now my ship—my home!

The USS *Liscome Bay* CVE 56 was the second vessel built in a new class of warship. It was labeled an escort carrier or baby carrier, smaller and more efficient than the much larger, standard-size aircraft carrier. Though it was called small, it took most of us several days to find our way from one compartment to another.

As I carried my belongings to my assigned compartment, many thoughts raced through my mind. "These are close quarters…. A lot of men will be sharing a very small space. Who will I work with? Who will I 'pal up' with? Will I remember what I have been taught … and respond as I should? Yes, I will!" I answered my question with firm determination. I came back to the task at hand and finished getting my things in order with a statement of reality: "I am on my way to the South Pacific Ocean to fight for the United States of America. War, here I come!"

"Get the hell off this ship!"

For almost four weeks, we added more crew members and loaded equipment and supplies. Every area of work was carefully checked to be sure all was in order and no further adjustments were necessary. We began a few practice runs and exercises in Puget Sound to test the ship. It was new, the crew was new. We needed to become acquainted with each other and the ship. It was extremely important that each sailor knew his job and could perform all his duties correctly.

We took more "shakedown" cruises in and around Puget Sound as well as exercise drills and became familiar with the ship and our responsibilities. Everyone practiced his duties aboard ship, from the galley to sleeping quarters, from communication to maintenance of the vessel. All OK!

From time to time more supplies and crew members were brought aboard ship. We had to be fully self-sufficient. The ship was not only our home, it was also our city. We had a post office, a barber shop, a laundry, anything we might need for days and possibly weeks. Everything had to be in place and ready to use.

Our first real-life practice exercise was September 7, 1943. The Liscome Bay left the dock at Astoria, Oregon, and cruised into the Columbia River Channel toward the Pacific Ocean. We were extremely excited to finally be headed out to sea! It was not long after reaching the ocean until many crew members lost their feeling of elation and were fighting sea sickness. Eating was not a pleasurable experience since the food did not stay down long. I was among the fortunate few who felt no ill effect from the constant rocking and rolling of the ship, however my sympathy went out to those who were sick with no possible relief. Many sailors could not even stand up, let alone perform their duties. Things got pretty bad before they got better.

The following day the ship anchored at Bremerton, Washington, and for two days all the crew worked at loading—carefully loading—boxes and crates of ammunition, hundreds of bombs of all sizes were stored for future use. Depth charges were stored in the ship's lowest level of the four story ship, along with other types of explosives. After all was safely and properly placed, we headed to a special area in the Puget Sound to be de-magnetized. Our next move was sailing back out to sea to test all our guns. The noise was deafening! This task was successfully completed and we returned to Seattle. Now, we were finally prepared to ship out to join the great United States Pacific fleet.

5

Practicing for Battle

On September 15, I wrote a short note to my family before a night out on the town with my buddies from the signal gang. I related my recent activities and ended the letter by saying, "Whatever happens, I am glad to be in the Navy. I'm happy with the choice I made."

An unusual problem was discovered on the *Liscome Bay* during its "shakedown" exercises. For some unknown reason the carrier had a permanent list of five degrees to starboard which could not be corrected. We affectionately called her "Listing Lizzie."

On September 17 the captain gave the order to head south to the Alameda Naval Air Station at San Francisco. The next day the *Liscome Bay* sailed into San Francisco Bay in all its glory, with the ship's company in dress uniform for all to see. For most of us it was the first time to see the famous Golden Gate Bridge and the pretty city of San Francisco. In the Bay we saw the island of Alcatraz, a curiosity to behold. Further into the Bay we passed under the Oakland Bridge before we docked at Alameda NAS.

For two days we stayed in dock while refueling and adding to our supplies, then we went on to San Diego, arriving there September 22. At this point we were transporting airplanes from one station to another. After unloading approximately sixty planes, the captain ordered the ship to sea for a final practice of night gunnery skills. The noise and flashing lights reminded me of the fireworks at the county fair back home.

We still needed a variety of training drills. Some were in heavy fog that had gathered in the San Diego area. It was difficult to see from one end of the ship to the other and we certainly could not see other ships or land. I'm not sure how many days we were anchored near Point Loma, where we listened to foghorns and clanging bells from nearby ships. It was an interesting experience.

While we were anchored at Point Loma, we learned we would be the flagship for our carrier division. Constructional changes were needed to

"Get the hell off this ship!"

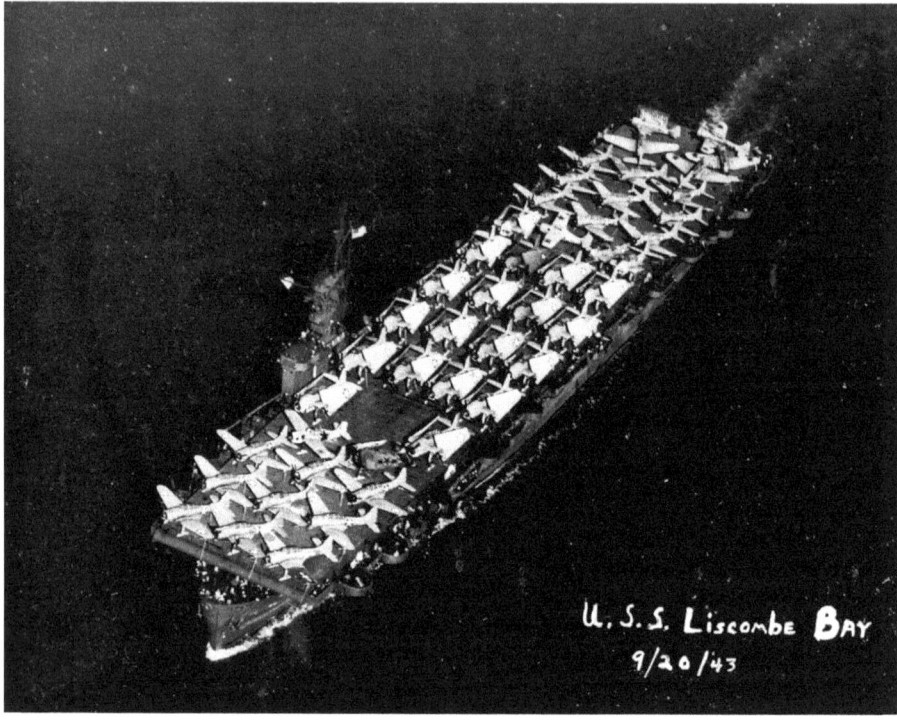

The *Liscome Bay* with Wildcat fighters and Avenger bombers on deck (Navy Archives).

house the rear admiral and his staff, so we spent several days at San Pedro Naval Base. The whole division would be commanded by Rear Admiral Henry M. Mullinnix from the *Liscome Bay*. Most of his staff were experienced, well-trained officers, highly respected in the Navy and worthy of their excellent reputation. We considered it a great honor to be chosen to serve these men.

October 14, the *Liscome Bay* received Wildcats, Hellcats, and Avengers on the flight deck. Each plane had its wings folded back and was taken by elevator (there were two on the ship) to the hanger deck below for storage. A total of twenty-eight fighters and bombers were placed aboard our "baby carrier" along with thirty-six officers and forty-one enlisted men. I was amazed as I watched all the planes and men take their assigned positions on the ship. Each fit into the special space allotted to them. Every nook and cranny was filled!

We were confident our American-built planes were superior to the

5. Practicing for Battle

enemy Japanese planes and that in battle we would be the victor. However, we also knew we had a serious problem: lack of training. Our pilots had not had the opportunity to practice take-offs and landings on a carrier, especially a carrier with a short runway like ours.

We headed out to sea again for the pilots to practice on our small landing deck. In spite of their good flying skills and excellent guidance by their crews, several pilots and planes were lost. Perfect timing and proper signaling played an important part in a successful flight. All aboard, the flight crew and the air crew saw firsthand the dangers they were facing. There were no instruments to guide the pilots. The decisions were made by the men involved. A thumbs-up signaled the pilot to blast off into the air. We called a landing on a carrier a "controlled crash."

While at sea, watching these practices, I began to realize more and more the seriousness of war. I witnessed my first casualty. On October 16, as a pilot guided his Wildcat toward the flight deck, he miscalculated the landing. He missed the final stopping cable and his fighter plane went over the starboard side, plunging into the water with a heavy splash. I was on signal duty on the bridge. I ran over to see the terrible accident.

I recognized the pilot as a lieutenant I had seen on deck several times. But I especially remembered seeing him board the *Liscome Bay* in San Diego. I watched him kiss his young wife and little baby good-bye and with great excitement wave to them as he came on board the ship. Now, in an instant, he was gone. I watched him struggling to free himself to get out of the plane but his Wildcat sank quickly. We were all in shock! There was absolutely nothing anyone could do to help. What a sad ending to a practice drill.

The atmosphere on the ship was somber. I—and I feel sure the others on the *Liscome Bay*—knew death was close by and would continue to follow us.

With heavy hearts we sailed back to San Diego, where we loaded up military supplies to be taken to the Hawaiian Islands. During the night of October 21, we left the dock at San Diego destined for Pearl Harbor. No time for a lump in the throat, only thoughts of the job we were assigned to do.

The baby carrier, *Liscome Bay*, sailed westward through the waters of the beautiful Pacific Ocean alone. We carried on with our daily routine duties, spent much time visiting and getting better acquainted with fellow sailors. I also spent time reflecting on the events of the past year—events good and bad—but who could be sad looking out at the blue water that surrounded our ship? Most days the sun shone brightly but there were also cloudy and

"Get the hell off this ship!"

stormy days. Sometimes the sparkling waves were high and rough but at other times they were almost nonexistent. The trade winds were ever-present to keep us cool and refreshed. We had no problem adjusting to the weather. Nights were special! Stars were everywhere, and the reflection of the moon on the water made it a crystal silver color.

We grew closer to one another as we spent more and more time becoming better acquainted. We were closer than brothers. A true comradeship existed as we shared our mail, our pasts and our hopes for our futures. The greatest difference among us was the language we spoke. In only a short time we recognized the Brooklyn accent, the southern drawl, the midwestern brogue and the far west dialect. Pete, a fellow signalman from Louisiana, spoke with a Cajun dialect and I with the Appalachian hillbilly accent, but we were the best of friends. We constantly corrected each other's pronunciation. One evening while on duty, Pete suddenly stood up and exclaimed, "Look at that big moon coming up over the horizon!" Very seriously I stated, "Pete, the word is hor'-i-zon, not ho-ri'zon!" He gave me a puzzled look but said nothing. A buddy agreed with me and we almost had him convinced he was wrong when a fourth buddy spoiled our joke by telling him we were only teasing.

A sense of humor was important to us in our overcrowded quarters. We shared many good-natured jokes in tense moments as well as in jovial times.

Everything seemed so peaceful. I relaxed and reminisced about my life back home. The thoughts of my boyhood on the farm with my family and my years in school seemed like a dream, or was I living in a dream now? Could I really be on a ship in the middle of the ocean with no land in sight, not knowing what would be ahead beyond all those miles of water? Truth was I liked it! I did not admit to myself that I was going into danger and not on vacation. Then, when I least expected it, the vision returned of the young pilot sinking below the water in his plane. Reality had a way of reappearing.

About halfway to Hawaii looking out at all the water, I smiled to myself as I remembered my water experience at age twelve. Our home was not far from a small river and my brothers and I went there to wade and play in the water. We gathered rocks and threw them into the deep part to watch the splash. While having fun, one thing led to another. We ended up getting wet from head to toe. Since we were already wet we might as well swim. Needless to say Mama was not happy with us when we got home. But it had been so much fun! We had a great idea—we could shave our heads, and with no

5. *Practicing for Battle*

bathing suits, we could take off our clothes. We did not want to give our secret away by having to go home naked so I took charge! We would alternate the duty of guarding our clothes. At the end of the summer, when we made our confessions, Mama told us she had suspected it but said nothing. That was the extent of my water adventure.

6

Hawaii

We spent four and a half days sailing from San Diego to the Hawaiian Islands, which at that time was a territory of the United States. All seemed to be going according to plan. No enemy planes or ships were sighted. At dusk on October 27 we dropped anchor off the island of Oahu. After a restful but anxious night we gathered at daybreak on the deck to get our first clear view of the area. Facing one direction we saw beautiful blue water, white sandy beaches with the rise of mountains in the distance. But in the opposite direction we saw only devastation caused by the Japanese attack. We were speechless.

Though the sneak attack had happened almost two years earlier, we saw remains of ships, planes and buildings. The entire military base was in ugly shambles. The United States had been occupied with the war and not a clean-up job. We tied up at Ford Island amidst the destruction. Hickman Field was nearby and a few planes were landing and taking off on the repaired runway.

Our crew members were granted leave to go ashore to see the famous Hawaiian Islands. What a strange feeling to walk on land again after being on a swaying ship for days. When we returned in the evening we were greeted with an unpleasant surprise. The dock workers had not taken the supplies off the ship that we had brought from the United States and our captain was furious! He loudly demanded, "Get these things off this ship and on the dock—in a hurry!" He may have made the request a little stronger and with more powerful words.

Though it took us several hours of hard labor, we finished the task to the satisfaction of the captain. He did not tell us but he was pleased with the way we worked together. At that moment, the crew of the *Liscome Bay* knew they were a good team and could be proud of their efforts.

We remained in dock for a week, getting some additional crew members on board and loading supplies we might need for an indefinite time. Just how long it would be before we docked in a friendly port, no one knew.

6. Hawaii

I frequently wrote to the family telling where I was and what I was doing. But now, I was out of the United States and in a war zone and all letters were being censored. I was told what I was permitted to tell folks at home and if I said too much it was blacked out. I remember how brief my letter was to Daddy: "All is well. I have arrived at a place in the Pacific Ocean. I can't tell you where but it is very nice, sunny and warm." I liked Hawaii a lot and took every opportunity to go on shore and wander around. There was beauty everywhere—unknown flowers and trees, the water and sand, all beyond description. It was not hard to find good food and drinks and very pretty, friendly girls.

Celebrating with friends in Hawaii. Jim Beasley front row, left.

While in the Hawaiian Islands, the *Liscome Bay* went through some more intense training. We would be traveling in a convoy, so formation practice was extremely important. All ships had a special position in the formation for protection during battle. We had three sister carriers and a number of other ships in our division. The air group tried to simulate, as nearly as possible, a fight with Japanese Zeroes. Our weather instruments and radios were tested for accuracy. The signal group practiced all means of their communication to improve speed and accuracy.

I was happy to practice my skills in sending and receiving messages. The officers constantly reminded us how important practice was in time of conflict. Soon it would not be merely practice but the real thing! After this training session we returned to Pearl Harbor totally exhausted.

"Get the hell off this ship!"

This was one occasion I recall we did not obey orders! A lone airplane approached overhead and signals were given for us to man our battle stations. Only a few responded to the call. Most of us were so exhausted we slept through all the alarms! No harm was done so there was no punishment.

While we were in Hawaii rumors circulated about our possible destination. The Aleutian Islands were mentioned. None of us believed that idea because we had not been issued cold-weather gear. There would be a lot of cold sailors to try to fight a war! The mystery kept us wondering and guessing.

The job of a ship's signalman was to send and receive messages of all kinds, secret or otherwise. Sometimes we used flag hoist or semaphore but usually a flashing light using Morse code. (The air group had its own corps of signalmen.) A member of our signal gang was always standing watch on the signal bridge ready to read any incoming messages and send a response. The mode of transmission depended on the present circumstances. There was no room for error. All signalmen were trained to spot and identify vessels on the water or aircraft in the sky. We could also assist the quartermaster. A signalman on duty was never idle.

The final supplies for our voyage were loaded on the *Liscome Bay* on November 10 and there was no need to tell us we would not be returning to port any time soon. That was obvious. Our task force gathered into the assigned formation. Ships were everywhere—battleships, cruisers, carriers, destroyers, transports and auxiliary ships. I learned later it was, up to that time, the largest and most powerful United States naval force ever assembled in the Pacific. It looked like the entire Navy to me!

In formation the *Liscome Bay* headed out into the unknown. Soon after leaving port, the captain announced our destination. Our large armada was headed to the Japanese-held Gilbert Islands to fight for its control and push out the enemy. I thought, "Where are the Gilbert Islands?" All I knew was they were located somewhere in the Pacific Ocean, a long way from Hawaii!

Thinking back, after the bombing of Pearl Harbor all the talk in our community had been about the war. In Europe the Allies fought against Germany and Italy, but halfway around the world in the Pacific, Japan was the enemy. I did not remember any places in particular but the Gilbert Islands seemed to have a familiar sound. When I came home from school or work, I joined the family listening to the radio for the latest news. Almost every evening we listened to Edward R. Murrow and Gabriel Heater to learn of the daily events. I paid little attention to specific names of places that were so far away they would never affect me—or so I thought!

6. Hawaii

I was upset that Germany's Hitler was grabbing one country after another in Europe. I thought Japan was terribly greedy trying to conquer China and many other parts of Asia. What a terrible situation, but that was not my problem—until Pearl Harbor—and now I was headed right into the midst of the conflict!

I racked my brain to remember places, people, and events I had heard mentioned on the news. I thought how serious President F.D. Roosevelt had been when he tried to warn the American people about the war getting closer and closer to us. We did not want to listen to his warnings of danger. Chiang Kai-shek of China and Winston Churchill of the United Kingdom were pleading for our help. We did not want to get involved in war. World War I had made us want to avoid another world war. It took the surprise attack on Pearl Harbor by Japan to wake us up to reality and force us to defend ourselves and help our friends.

The slogan "Remember Pearl Harbor" was everywhere and it stirred the country to action. For the next few months after December 7, 1941, all the news from both war zones was discouraging. The United States was not prepared for a battle of any kind, and what limited military personnel and supplies we had were destroyed in Hawaii. General Douglas MacArthur had some defenses in the Philippine Islands but the Japanese were overpowering him there.

I remember hearing of a few other Islands—Guam, Saipan, Wake, Marshall, and the Gilbert Islands. That was where I was headed! What had happened to them, and where were they located? These questions would soon be answered. I was now leaving Hawaii and heading to the group of islands known as the Gilbert Islands, aboard the *Liscome Bay* with the fighting United States Navy.

Admiral Chester Nimitz headed up the 5th Fleet and under his command was Vice Admiral Raymond Spruance. We were under his direct command. Both men were well-respected and highly-decorated Navy heroes. I was proud to be under the command of such outstanding and devoted leaders. I was also proud of the United States Navy of which I was a part.

7

Fun and Fight

After we spent a few days back at sea sailing westward, our work began to be routine. Each of us fulfilled our duties with no problems. We worked, ate, slept and felt like a family who needed each other to make things go smoothly. Despite our different childhood backgrounds, we were really basically the same at heart. We discussed having the same goal: defeat the Japanese at all costs!

I recall the loud noise on November 12, as the gunnery crews practiced to perfect their skills. The pilots took off from the deck of the ship, flew a test patrol and landed again. They had a good and successful practice run. All these actions looked and sounded like war to me. On November 15 during a routine patrol, a fighter pilot took off in his Wildcat and plunged straight into the water with a stalled engine. He was unable to escape and went down with his plane. I had witnessed another terrible tragedy. With our real feelings suppressed, we said little but continued on with the job at hand. In most situations the Wildcat lived up to its good name but there were occasional mishaps.

November 16 was a day for a traditional celebration! Preparations were being made for Neptune's Party. I had heard the older sailors tell of a long-held tradition when the seasoned "shellbacks" invited (commanded) the newcomers or "pollywogs" to a party when they crossed the 180th Meridian for the first time. As for this crew on the *Liscome Bay* most aboard the ship were pollywogs. We were all excited, not knowing what the party would be like.

We gathered on deck, and after about thirty minutes, King Neptune and his court appeared. The king told us it was time for all pollywogs to enter into the "Solemn Mysteries of the Ancient Order of the Deep." After the barber, using some kind of aviator shears, began shaving our heads, a fuel oil mixture was poured over us. Next, they turned the fire hose on us and dropped us into a tank of water—blindfolded! That was the fun part. Some of us were forced to eat terrible mixtures of strange food. Some received an

7. Fun and Fight

electric shock, while others were covered with paint. Whatever the shellbacks had planned, we had to do. Lastly, there was a long line of shellbacks with paddles waiting for us to run down the line. Each man seemed to hit harder with a long paddle than the previous man. Somehow I managed to get through the line on both feet. We all survived with the vow "Just wait until I get to act the shellback role!" I was given a card from the "Imperial Domain of the Golden Dragon" saying I had been inducted into the "Silent Mysteries of the Far East." When the good-natured fun ended, the decks were cleared and we got back to business with a deeper feeling of devotion to ship, each other and our mission. The light-hearted fun was good for our morale.

We were now entering the area of possible danger and each day brought some special event. On November 17, our patrols and exercises were for real, not just practice. On November 18, the captain made a serious announcement over the loud speaker for all to hear. I remember well the essence of his message: "This is the captain. We are going to attack the Gilbert Islands. We will be the air support for the United States forces of invasion on the Island of Makin. I'm sure every man will do his job and do it well. We will hit the Japanese with everything we have, day and night, until the job is done. That is

The *Liscome Bay* crew celebrating crossing the 180th meridian.

all." There was a loud cheer of approval. This would be our first battle aboard the *Liscome Bay*!

The Gilbert Islands, especially Makin, became part of our daily conversation. The knowledge and anticipation of the impending battle helped us continue to practice and review our skills with more dedication. At this time our patrol planes did not report any sightings of the enemy. Our greatest excitement on board was the illness of one of the crew members, an emergency appendectomy. One very disheartened sailor was placed in sick bay for recovery.

On November 19, very early in the morning, the island of Makin in the Gilbert Islands appeared. We received a report of enemy aircraft nearby and our agile fighter planes, the Wildcats, took off to search for them. However, that turned out to be a false alarm.

On November 20, the action began for real! Makin Island was heavily shelled by support ships before any troops or equipment were sent on to the beach. At this time and location there was little Japanese resistance but the sights and sounds told us we were not conducting a practice. Our planes were flying through the visible sky area. The battleships ahead of us were blasting away. We could see black smoke and bright flames coming from Makin Island even though we were on the outer edge of the convoy. There were several very large explosions. As our gunfire slowed and the response from the enemy seemed to cease, more and more troops landed on the beach. It was several hours before all gunfire stopped.

The beaches of Makin proved to be far from an ideal landing place for an invasion. Soldiers struggled onto the coral reef. Their equipment was often stranded behind them at the edge of the water. The operation went much slower than had been anticipated. Throughout the landing process our planes flew overhead, searching for the enemy on shore, in the air and from submarines in the water. The *Liscome Bay* was close enough to Makin for us to see the devastation our planes and ships had inflicted on the island. All the vegetation was gone. The whole area looked like a real battle zone, which it was!

Tragedy struck us again as we were praising ourselves for our part in the battle. A young pilot took off for patrol duty and cleared the end of the ship but never came up into sight again. The engine failed and the plane landed on the water. Luckily, two crew members got out safely but one went down with the plane.

As war activities continued and I looked around me at all the ships and

7. Fun and Fight

men involved, I could hardly believe I was in the middle of such a situation. Was I really in a world war, in the Pacific Ocean thousands of miles from home, on an aircraft carrier fighting in the United States Navy, or was it a dream? The statement that had flashed into my mind so many times popped up again—"I am only eighteen years old!"

After our first real-live battle, the night of November 20 was an anxious time for all on the *Liscome Bay*. We knew anything could happen. However, we thought we were prepared for what might come our way and felt confident of the progress made in the capture of Makin Island. We continued our duties and kept alert hoping tomorrow would be less active and not so stressful.

November 21 was another day to show our power and strong intentions to win the conflict. Most of the efforts of the Army and Navy were to be praised but sometimes a mistake can occur, as it did on this day.

Poor communications were believed to be the cause of a mistake which resulted in the death of some of our own men. I did not personally know anyone involved but the event hit me hard. As a signalman I knew the difficulty in trying to coordinate the plans of air troops and ground troops. I was aware of how a simple error could result in tragedy. Our training and equipment could not assure a successful exchange of messages in all situations. The importance of accuracy in my job was making a lasting impression.

We were on a working schedule of four hours on duty and four hours off. On November 22, my four-hour watch began at twelve midnight and ended at four in the morning. Pete Umbehagan and I reported on time, got the report from those leaving their watch, poured a cup of good hot coffee and sat down hoping for a peaceful watch. I noticed Pete was unusually quiet. As he came over and sat beside me, he said, "I want to talk to you." I responded, "OK—what do you want to talk about?" It was obvious he had a serious matter to discuss.

He told me he was scared and very concerned about a recent dream he had and he could not get it off his mind. He began, "The two of us were on duty on a dark night with choppy seas—like tonight. I looked up and saw a strange white creature coming down the radar mast. I pointed it out to you and asked if you could see it too. You said you could." Pete continued, "This thing came closer to us. It was a faceless man dressed in a white robe. You asked, 'Who are you and what do you want?' It answered you, 'I'm the Grand Reaper. My name is Death. I have come for both of you!' I was scared!"

Pete was excited and very nervous as he told the account of his dream. He said when we argued with the creature and threatened it, the thing slowly

"Get the hell off this ship!"

moved away and climbed back up the mast. Upon reaching the top, it turned and said, "You wait and see—I will be back!" I tried to convince Pete it was only a foolish dream but I had to admit it was strange and disturbing. We went on with our work duty.

November 22 was the third day of the invasion of Makin Island and our troops were moving slowly in their forward advance for several reasons. First, the heat was almost unbearable, second, the heavy undergrowth blocked any rapid movement, and third, the Japanese resistance had stepped up. Taking possession of the island was quite a struggle.

On the *Liscome Bay*, we retained our position, carrying out our support efforts of flying combat air patrols as well as anti-submarine patrols. We were aware of the large number of enemy subs in the area and knew they were the greatest threat to our ship. Remaining in one position, we were an obvious sitting target.

On this day we suffered a minor loss. A pilot coming in for a landing could not lower his plane's tail hook. However, he succeeded in landing his plane in a nearby lagoon. He and his crew were rescued by an amtrac vehicle from the island. Only the plane was lost.

On November 23 at 10:30 we received a welcome message; it said simply, "Makin taken!" We wanted to celebrate. Our first real encounter in war had been a success. Japan had expected us to strike in another location and they were unprepared for battle at Makin. Lady luck was with us. We were a happy group of men!

8

Calm Before the Storm

The Makin Island mission for the *Liscome Bay* was now successfully completed and we were headed back out to sea. We expected our operation aboard ship to be routine—general quarters, flight quarters, planes taking off and landing, and taking on fuel and ammunition, the usual thing to do after a battle. At this point we were some distance from Makin and the ground battle was being fought on the island. We continued to receive information on the progress being made by our troops there. News came of the difficulties the Marines were facing during their invasion of Tarawa, a sister island in the Gilberts. Our orders were to spend four hours on watch and four hours off duty on a continuous basis. We were making every effort to be safe in a dangerous situation and location.

Why, I do not know, but my parents always called me by my middle name, Claude. So from birth I was Claude Beasley. In December 1942 when I entered the Navy, I became James or Jim, and my whole life changed—even my name. For almost a year now, I had been a sailor in the U.S. Navy, answering to a new name, learning new skills, and traveling halfway around the world. Everything was moving so fast!

As for my name, when I was in boot camp and also in signalman school, I was "Hey you!" or simply "Sailor." The name had little meaning as we would be together for only a short time. When I came on board the *Liscome Bay*, it was different because we expected to be together for a long time.

A name was important to identify each person as someone special. We knew we would eat, sleep, play, work, and talk together. Many of us picked up a nickname. I became Sam! Who pinned that on me I do not know. Of course, officially, I was Beasley. The officers addressed the men by last name only, but to friends I was more than Beasley, I was Sam.

We had now been on board the *Liscome Bay* for more than three months and we were becoming better acquainted with each other and our ship. I had many very good friends in the signal gang and several from other groups. It

"Get the hell off this ship!"

had become easier to recognize and properly address our officers. I thought all of them were sincerely dedicated and well trained to perform their duties. We had great respect for all our superior officers and had no trouble following orders. The chaplain and the doctor were always ready with a helping hand. I knew I was with the best group of men who ever served on a ship in the entire Navy. We also had the distinction of being chosen to be the flagship of our division. What an honor to have the rear admiral on board with us. Was I a lucky fellow, or what?

On the morning of November 23, a friend in the signal gang and I went top side to sit on the catwalk near the bags of signal flags. We were relaxing and waiting for chow time. I was reading *Moby Dick* and my friend Chester R. Williams fell asleep. Just before noon I shook my friend to wake him.

I told him, "Chuck, it's time to get ready for chow." He replied, "Sam, I wish I could have slept longer, so I could finish my dream." Then he began to tell me about the good dream I had interrupted.

"It was a wonderful dream, Sam. The war was over and I was back in Alabama. Oh, it was such a beautiful day! I was home on my family's farm with my girlfriend and we were planning our wedding. I had invited all the signal gang from the *Liscome Bay* to a party to announce our plans. Everyone was having a great time, but I could not find you. I went through the whole crowd, but could not find you anywhere. I wanted you to meet my girl, my wife-to-be, and I also owed you $20. While looking for you I discovered there were four other signalmen who were missing." Williams stopped talking and seemed to be thinking. On the way to chow he named the other four missing signalmen and we briefly discussed his dream. He said how happy the dream made him. We dismissed our thoughts and went below to eat.

Several more ships were added to our group and the whole task force grew in number. We were ready and waiting for new orders to leave the present dangerous location. All on board knew it was just a matter of time until the Japanese made their move to get our carrier.

In the late afternoon we received the warning of enemy submarines only a short distance away. Quickly five planes took off from our ship to find the nearby submarines. In only fifteen minutes we had lost contact with all five of the Wildcats. Had they sighted real danger, we did not know—they were lost to us. Several other ships tried to get in touch with them but were also unsuccessful. It was getting late in the day and the sky was darkening with an approaching storm. Could the pilots find the *Liscome Bay*? Could they make a landing after dark?

8. Calm Before the Storm

In the anxious moments that followed, many crew members stayed on deck listening to the increasing winds as the sky darkened, looking for some sign of the returning planes. We had no doubt our pilots, with some good luck, could bring the planes down on the water, get into life rafts and be rescued in tomorrow's daylight. We must get on with our duties and get a little sleep, as we were already on a four-hour shift and tomorrow would certainly bring another busy day.

(A few days later we learned our pilots had realized the danger of the approaching storm and had gotten permission to land on other carriers. Four of the Wildcats had landed on the big carrier *Yorktown* and the other plane landed on the big carrier *Lexington*. All were safe!)

The ships in our task force were preparing to move out of the area, and since the *Liscome Bay* was the flagship, she was in the center of the formation. The signalmen were busy with a variety of means of communication with other ships. The escort carriers were placed inside of a circular formation because they were not capable of defending themselves. Constructed with a "thin skin," not reinforced for safety, they were very vulnerable in an attack. Some of our protective vessels had been called out of formation and were hurrying to get back to their designated position. All the while we were moving forward. The holes in the outer circle were being closed but would it be soon enough. As we moved along we received several warnings of unidentified aircraft and were also on constant alert looking for enemy submarines. It was a busy and stressful evening and night. As I went on with my duties I recalled the two recent dreams of my fellow signalmen. I thought to myself, "Why such strange and unusual dreams?"

9

Tragedy

The next morning, November 24, at 3:45 a.m., I was drinking a cup of coffee in the signal shack and getting a report from the previous signalman who had been on duty. He reported all was well. At 4:00 a.m., settling in for my watch on the bridge, I learned there was still no report from our five missing patrol planes. Officers were stirring around when "Reveille" sounded at 4:30. I noticed the crescent moon on the horizon. I felt the balmy breeze with a temperature of a nice 82 degrees and everything seemed to be calm and quiet. At 5:05 general quarters sounded and each man reported to his battle station. This was the normal morning routine in a war area because it's the best time for the enemy to make a surprise attack.

The captain was on the bridge with other officers. From my duty post I could see them and almost everything that happened on the open deck. I left the bridge momentarily to go below to make certain all the signalmen were awake. I went down a special escape hatch and ladder the captain had recently ordered constructed on deck. I met a fellow signalman coming up the ladder who assured me all of our men were up and moving about. I returned to my duty post on the bridge. Officers and seamen were in proper position for whatever came our way—so we thought.

The morning became unusually dark and the sky had an eerie appearance. I had a strange feeling inside, as if something big was about to happen.

The admiral was talking with other officers and making plans for the day. I watched the flight crews prepare the planes for takeoff as each pilot double checked his plane. I was chatting with the chief of the signal crew and another signal officer who was a lieutenant. Ships were still zigzagging from side to side trying to resume their correct position. Suddenly, the *Liscome Bay* was hit by a torpedo! One of the crew members had spotted the torpedo before it hit and yelled, "TORPEDO!" It was too late and only a few men on the ship could hear him.

The torpedo struck the ship in the worst possible place. It hit the space

9. Tragedy

below deck where the aircraft bomb magazine was located. Immediately after the loud boom of the torpedo explosion came other loud booms. Bombs began to explode in the magazine and ammunition went off everywhere. Fires broke out on all levels. Airplanes exploded as fuel tanks caught fire. It was a flaming inferno!

I was thrown backward from the first explosion but quickly picked myself up. The after part of the flight deck had been opened up and I could see down into the entire bowels of the *Liscome Bay*. When I looked down into the hole where the flight deck had been, I saw nothing but blazing fire. "That looks like hell!" I thought. Since my grandfather was a Free Will Baptist preacher, I knew from his description this was hell itself! The terrible scene is impossible to describe. Many of my buddies were down there.

The jolts from the explosions caused flaming planes to shoot off the remaining deck, while other planes burned in place. Who was inside the planes? I stood there in a daze before my training kicked in. I automatically rushed over to help the bugler and a boatswain who were trapped beneath the fallen radar antenna, which had missed me by a hair when it fell. I could not move the heavy metal pole but others helped me slide it off the men. Neither man moved—they were gone. I knew the bugler personally. One-third of the ship was destroyed, and the rest was on fire. "Just how long can the *Liscome Bay* stay afloat?" I said to myself.

The stark contrast of darkness all around and bright fires burning on our ship hindered the view of the many ships in the convoy. At the moment, we had to go it alone; no one was able to help. We were totally helpless sitting in the ocean with no water to try to extinguish the fire. The smell of gas and oil was stifling. Passageways were blocked with debris or flames. Many men lay dead all around and the wounded were calling for help. Those who were able tried to find a way to escape as the ship began to list badly to one side. The heat was so intense even the guns in different parts of the ship were firing. Planes continued to explode. In the confusion, I heard someone yell, "Get the hell off this ship!" I did not know if that was a command or merely an obvious observation. I looked at the lifeless bodies all around me and thought, "So far I have survived—why? I am eighteen and tomorrow, November 25, I'll be nineteen—will I make it?"

It seemed the explosions would not end as ammunition and bombs continued to ignite. The sounds were deafening but the moans and yells of the men could still be heard. When the stockpile of gun ammunition went off, it was like a giant popcorn popper. With stairwells blocked, ropes

"Get the hell off this ship!"

were used by those who were able to get from one level to another. Many men who were able to help sought out the injured and tried to get them to a safer location. Crew members were jumping into the water, some without their life jackets.

The ship was leaning on its side, so it was unsafe to jump into the water from the high side, but jumping in from the low side was even less safe. As the ship sank it could suck a swimmer down into the water with it. There was no safe place, either on board or in the water.

I had been standing on the bridge when the torpedo hit the ship and the force of the explosion blew the bridge to smithereens. I was wearing a helmet which blew off my head and my clothes were in shreds. I felt sharp pains in my ribs and stomach. My left shoe was torn open exposing my little toe which was dangling by only a piece of skin. But as I looked around I knew I was in good shape.

Terrible destruction and injured men lay all around me. I gazed at the bodies of the bugler and boatswain who were killed by the fallen radio antenna pole. It had taken super strength for me, Lt. Gardner Smith and another man to move the pole from on top of them. I scanned the area before moving on. I felt a deep sadness for those young men, many of whom were friends or acquaintances, but many I did not know. I was thankful to be alive and well! There was work to be done—quickly!

My life jacket was in the signal shack behind me. I turned and tried to open the door but it was jammed shut. I heard a voice inside frantically calling, "Open the door!" I looked around and found a metal rod lying nearby on the deck. I hammered and hammered on the latches with the rod. Finally the door opened and two buddies from the signal gang rushed out; both were wearing their life jackets. I grabbed mine and quickly slipped it on while running over to the area where the captain usually stood. He was not there.

Fire, smoke and the ship's rubble blocked the exits to the bridge area. In a nearby smoke-filled compartment I could barely see the form of a man slumped over the desk. When I called out to him there was no answer. I went over to him and lifted his arm. The lifeless arm fell back on the desk with a thud. What could I do? In the smoky darkness I could not see well enough to identify the man. Could this be the admiral? I had seen him near this area just before the torpedo struck. There was nothing I could do to help him. Something told me, "Get moving, Beasley!"

I began going through all the dark compartments to see if there was anyone who needed help when I met up with the lieutenant commander. I

9. Tragedy

said to him, "Sir, you seem to be the senior officer on the bridge, tell us what we should do!"

"Abandon ship and get off as quickly as possible!" was his immediate reply.

"Yes, sir!" I said as I began to move forward. Two fellow signal officers had heard the order and asked me if I knew a way off the ship. "Yes, I do, follow me." I led the two men down the escape hatch the captain had ordered constructed only days before. I had used it that very morning. This brought us to the flight deck which was surrounded by hot flames. We seemed to be trapped with no way to get through the fire.

I knew there were some long lines of rope in the catwalk and with the two men, Lieutenant Glenn Hunt and Chief Signalman Lloyd Luzani, following me, we located the container which housed the lines. We opened the lid, got out the lines and threw them over the side of the ship.

One of the two men with me went down first and called back, "Come on down!" I grabbed a rope and jumped over the side. I quickly climbed hand-over-hand down the rope. Suddenly, I couldn't move. My life jacket had gotten caught on a piece of metal on the ship. I twisted, pulled and said a few choice words but could not free myself. While I was hanging about forty feet above the water, the other fellow climbed over the top of me and down the rope into the water. I always carried a sheath knife on my belt in case of an emergency—this was an emergency! I took it out, cut my life jacket loose and continued to climb down to the choppy water. The two men were gone. I assumed they had made it down successfully and had moved on. When I later checked the survivor list, their names were not there. I have pondered over the situation. To this day, I wonder if that piece of metal on the ship that caught my life jacket and delayed my ascent actually saved my life.

The surface of the water was covered with oil, which was on fire and burning fiercely. When I reached the bottom of the rope to jump into the ocean, I found a man hanging on to the end of the rope and screaming. I did not know him, but he needed help. Terrified, he continued to holler, "I can't swim. I can't swim!"

Yelling above the noise, I hollered back, "I can swim well, hold onto my life jacket!" He grabbed the edge of the jacket and held on tightly. Not only was the water burning, flaming globs of oil from the deck were dripping on our heads. When my hair caught fire, I ducked under water to extinguish the blaze. As I lifted my head out of the water, I looked back at the ship to see it listing toward us. A scary sight!

"Get the hell off this ship!"

I had gone only a short distance from the ship when the terrified sailor began to panic. I tried to grab him but he fought loose and made his way back to the dangling rope. I swam back to him and tried to convince him we could make it together. He only screamed, "No, I can't swim and I don't have a life jacket." He refused to turn loose of the rope. I could see the ship going lower in the water and the fires on the water coming closer to us. What I had to tell him will be on my mind all my life. "If you won't come with me, I have no choice but to leave you. Good-bye and good luck." I felt terribly bad but I quickly turned and swam as hard as I could away from the sinking ship, leaving my shipmate behind, still clinging to the rope.

I kicked off my shoes, took off my torn, burnt clothes, to be able to move more quickly to safety away from my burning and sinking home. The *Liscome Bay* was sinking fast, literally disappearing into the ocean. Suddenly, there was an underwater explosion. It felt like my insides exploded with the terrible blast. After several more loud explosions, I thought I might lose consciousness. There was throbbing in my ears and my insides felt like they had shaken loose from my body. I hurt and everything seemed to be closing in on me. I knew I must have bruises all over, including my head which ached from ear to ear. My head was bald, as the hair had been singed by the burning oil on the top of the water.

In the darkness, still surrounded by burning fires, I was trying to swim away from the disaster and the danger. It was a struggle for me to stay alert but I kept on telling myself, "Survive! You must survive!" After swimming and swimming, I thought the ship must be far behind me now. As I turned to look, I realized the wind and currents were actually pushing the sinking ship toward me. Thoughts raced through my mind: "I can't swim faster than that ship is moving. When it goes down, I go with it!" I knew I had to change my direction and swim further to the side so the wind would be pushing the ship away from me.

I managed to get a safe distance from the ship and I sadly watched her last struggling moments. The *Liscome Bay* gave up her fight. The water had rapidly flooded all the compartments on every deck as she leaned to starboard. Stern first she sank beneath the water with ammunition still blasting inside of her. On the way down she continued to burn and I could hear the sizzling as the water came in contact with all the hot metal on board. Next, I saw a cloud of steam cover the surface of the water. Underneath the water the fire produced a deep orange glow. Then all was dark and she could be seen no more. She went down to her grave on the ocean floor.

9. Tragedy

It had been less than half an hour since I was standing at my signal station preparing for a day of action—but not this much! According to Naval Records the *Liscome Bay* sank in only twenty-three minutes, undoubtedly the worse twenty-three minutes of my life!

10

Survival

After I left the ship, struggling in the darkness to stay afloat, my thoughts seemed to be out of control. From positive thoughts, I would jump to negative thoughts and back again to positive. I constantly reminded myself, "I'm alive! I'm floating in the Pacific Ocean without a ship but I'm alive!" The last few months flashed before me: I had boarded the *Liscome Bay* and found I loved being on the water and sailing the ocean blue. The beautiful sea and skies fascinated me. But now the ocean was different, so big and lonely. No ship under me, no shipmates to talk to, what a difference in such a short time. I had little hope of making it through the tragedy and knew only a miracle could save me, but I also knew miracles happen every day. I forced myself to think, "I cannot let fear and doubt rule my life, but I do need help!" I asked myself, "Is God with me?" Then I answered my question with "Not if I give up!"

I wondered about my friends from the ship; had any of them survived? I thought of the officers who were older men and had families, wives and children at home waiting for them to return. "Don't dwell on sad thoughts, it consumes too much energy." But I continued to think without a lot of control over my mind. My family and good times at home flashed before me. "What if I don't make it out alive? Stop! Erase those thoughts from your mind, now!" In times like this it is very difficult but important to gain control of your every thought—a fact that could save your life.

Though it was still dark, soon after I went into the water I had a streak of good luck. Just when exhaustion seemed so close, a large object three feet by three feet and about four inches thick came floating toward me and brushed my arm. I felt of it and decided it was a piece of cork from the ship's refrigeration unit. It floated! I grabbed hold of it before it could get out of my reach and held on. My whole body was tired and now I could let my muscles rest. The first miracle had arrived in answer to my prayer for help.

As I rested my body and mind, I realized I was not alone. There were

10. Survival

cries of pain and yells of fear from my fellow crew members around me. Some came from a distance but others appeared to be very close. I saw a dark object and reached out to touch it. A severely wounded sailor was struggling to keep afloat as he dropped in and out of a state of consciousness. He was mumbling and calling for help, while crying in pain. I helped him take hold of my lifesaver, the large piece of cork. Then I wrapped my legs around his body in case he let go of our float in his fade-away moment. I was not able to see the extent of his injuries but I knew he was in very bad shape. I hoped he could make it with my help. Now I had two reasons to continue to survive. As he struggled to hang on to the cork and life, I was witnessing the end of the ship that had been my home.

I sadly commented, "There goes *the Liscome Bay*." In a very faint and weak voice, my companion added, "Good-bye." In the midst of the floating oil and debris we held on but said little. What was there to say? Our circumstances said it all. The surrounding sounds were fading away. Was I losing control of my senses? Or were we floating further away? I did not like either option.

The appearance of daylight was most welcome. I could see clearly the terrible condition of my new friend and I could understand the reason for his pain. He had been scalded! He was a steward working in the galley when the ship was hit and had been burned by hot grease. Each arm was one big blister, swollen and full of liquid. Not only was his head burned, but had a cut so deep I could actually see his skull. I constantly talked to him. "Hang on, Buddy, we will make it together." I hoped that would prove to be true.

I was relieved when three other swimmers joined us. They were floating on a large plank of wood from the flight deck. The plank was a much better support for my burned companion, and the men were also very helpful in taking care of him. All we could do was stay afloat, stay alive and in our right minds, and hope and pray to be rescued.

We could see destroyers in the area and knew there was someone out there looking for survivors. Help was on the way! What a boost to our morale. We watched as small boats pulled men from the water and took them to the rescue ship. We observed this time after time. We realized we were in a current that was taking us away from the other survivors but we yelled and hoped we had been spotted. No boats came in our direction—had they not seen us? Finally, our hopes sinking that the rescue effort was over, a boat appeared to be headed toward us. It was from the destroyer *Hughes* and was coming closer and closer. We made all the hollering noises and signs we could to be certain they saw us. There was no doubt they were headed directly for us! After three hours in the water we were being rescued by some of the Navy's angels. We laughed and cried at the same time. I thought, "This is another miracle in answer to my prayer."

11

Rescued

We climbed or were helped onto the boat and were taken to the rescue ship *Hughes*. As I stood on the deck I could hardly contain myself. I hurt, but looking at so many seriously wounded men, I thought my injuries were minor and of no real serious consequences. The ship began to move on. Were we the last to be picked up? Are there no more to rescue? As I looked out to sea I wondered, "Could we be leaving anyone out there to perish in the water? That had almost been my fate but now I am safe, and very, very thankful!" Again the thought came to mind, "What an experience in one year, I'm only eighteen. Will I make it until tomorrow, November 25, 1943, my nineteenth birthday?"

On the destroyer *Hughes*, the crew members were scurrying around trying to help the survivors of the *Liscome Bay*. The ship resembled a hospital ship with cots set up in every available compartment, in the hallways and on deck. It was a pitiful sight but no one complained. The overcrowded conditions were only a minor inconvenience as the sailors patiently waited for treatment. After all, it was great to be on board a ship and not still floating in the ocean!

My new friend, the badly-burned black steward, passed out as soon as he was lifted from the small boat and placed on the *Hughes*. A corpsman gave him a shot of morphine to ease his pain. As I looked at him I knew if he lived that would be another miracle.

In a daze, I stood on deck with no clothes on except a pair of ragged undershorts. My hair was burned off my head, my little toe was hanging by a sliver of skin and every time I breathed I coughed in pain. The corpsman with the needles filled with morphine came over to me and calmly said, "You're next." I quickly stepped back and said, "No thank you, sir, I'll make it without that stuff!" He wasted no time with me and moved on to attend to others. I did not want to be stuck with a dose of something that might put me to sleep. I wanted to stay awake and know I was alive.

"Get the hell off this ship!"

Wandering around the various places on the ship, I went to the mess hall and found they were handing out sandwiches and soup. I knew I needed a little nourishment but food was not appealing to me at that time. A part of the eating area was made into an infirmary, and the sights, sounds and stench were unbearable, so I moved on. I felt as if I might pass out if I remained there. I went back on the deck where I could breathe better air. I sat down in the shade of a five-inch gun and admitted to myself I was in some form of shock.

I realized that every move I had made since the first explosion on board the *Liscome Bay* had been an automatic response from my training, but now, I needed to refuel my mind and think! I didn't have any duties aboard the rescue ship. I was their guest. I was going to rest and get well.

Sitting there, relatively alone, I thought through the events of the day. There were too many happenings to process them at this time. I knew we were still in a dangerous situation but I felt safe. I understood we were moving out of the area as quickly as possible but the submarine that sank the *Liscome Bay* had not been located yet. It was somewhere underwater waiting to strike again. Would we be the target? Could another ship be sunk from under me? That is not a likely possibility. "Come on, Beasley! Get moving!"

For the first time since my rescue, I looked at myself and realized I needed some clothes. I went down to the ship's store to find most of the clothes had already been given out to my shipmates. I wore a size twenty-eight-waist dungaree and they were all gone. I ended up with a size forty undershorts with a rope to tie them around my waist. That was better than the ragged, oil-stained pair I was wearing. There were no shoes at all, so I settled for a size eleven overshoe. I normally wore a size eight shoe. I got two rubber bands to hold them on my feet and protect me from the hot deck. At this point, appearance was not very important to me or anyone else. I was alive and reasonably well-off physically.

The word went around that the destroyer *Hughes* was on the way back to Makin Island's lagoon where the *Liscome Bay* survivors would be transferred to another ship and taken to the hospital in Pearl Harbor. Going back to Hawaii sounded great. I did not know how many *Liscome Bay* survivors were on the *Hughes*, but they were all recognizable by appearance. Most of them I did not know by name, but we were all buddies. We were told two or three other vessels helped with the rescue and I hoped my friends in the signal gang had been among those survivors.

When we reached Makin Island we boarded a United States Coast Guard

11. Rescued

attack transport, the *Leonard Wood*, and were soon in route to Pearl Harbor. We were sailing with another transport ship also carrying survivors of the *Liscome Bay*. On the way we signaled each other the names of the lucky men on board each transport. By the end of the messages, it was determined more than six hundred men had been lost in the sinking of the *Liscome Bay*. That was not surprising. It was certainly a big loss and a sad time for those who did survive. I did not yet know who in my signal gang were among the survivors.

Next day, November 25, 1943, was Thanksgiving Day and I knew I had a lot to be thankful for. It was also my birthday. I had reached nineteen! Thinking over the last twelve months I could hardly comprehend all the events that had taken place in my life. I had joined the Navy and had boot camp training at Great Lakes Naval Training Station and several months of signal school at Farragut Naval Training Station in Idaho. I had been to Seattle, Portland, San Francisco, San Diego and Pearl Harbor before ending up in the islands of the Pacific. I had made new friends from all regions of the United States and I had learned many new skills. All the while I was having a great time. Then the sudden tragedy that war brings came in an instant—fighting to survive, or death! War is worse than you can imagine. You have to live it and experience the horror to realize the real truth. As I recalled these events I realized I was actually talking out loud! Anyone who heard me knew my mind was working under great stress.

"Today is my birthday and I will celebrate life!" I told myself as well as anyone who wanted to listen. Only a few days ago I had joked with another signalman. We were talking on the *Liscome Bay* and I asked him if he knew why we had hundreds of turkeys cooking in the galley. He quickly replied, "Of course, Thursday is Thanksgiving." I said, "No, my birthday is Thursday and they are for my party." We both laughed happily. I wondered if we would have turkey aboard the *Leonard Wood* for Thanksgiving Day.

What a Thanksgiving Day! What a happy birthday! I was extremely glad to be among the living and on a ship headed for Hawaii. I did not need a big party, cake, ice cream and presents, only the knowledge I would be around for awhile longer. It was a day of thanksgiving!

While still aboard the *Hughes* we were well cared for and well fed. She was a tough destroyer with a great crew. I struggled to face reality and look fate squarely in the eye. So much had been lost beyond my personal loss. I did not understand it but I knew I must accept the obvious facts. Also on the *Leonard Wood* we were treated with great respect and cared for in the best

"Get the hell off this ship!"

possible way. I had nothing to complain about, only praise for my fellow sailors. Thanks to all my brothers!

I had not heard what was happening in the Gilbert Islands. I wondered how our carrier division was without its flagship. Who was giving commands with the rear admiral gone? Who would replace our respected leader? I only knew my great ship, the *Liscome Bay*, had been sunk with so many good men on board on its first combat operation. Together we had rejoiced when victory at Makin was announced but the celebration was cut short by a Japanese submarine's successful torpedo.

I began to think of the individuals with whom I had the privilege of performing my daily tasks during the few months we had been together. As a signalman I had close association with most officers and had gained respect for each one. I had great admiration for them personally and professionally. They were and would remain my heroes.

Rear Admiral H. M. Mullinnix was a kind and friendly man and a knowledgeable, experienced and courageous seaman. Our ship's captain, I. D. Wiltsie, also a great military leader, once stated that the chaplain's job was the second most important job on the ship. He always praised and gave credit to others.

Our executive officer, Commander Finley Hall, was a good and likeable Southerner. I remember him saying in his Alabama drawl when he first sighted Makin Island, "There she is!" He announced the upcoming battle with enthusiasm and anticipation. He lost his life attempting to save his crew members who were trapped below deck. He rushed down to them and never returned. He left a young wife and a nine-year-old daughter.

There were also many heroes among the survivors.

Lieutenant Commander John Rowe, Senior Medical Officer, was our ever-present thirty-year-old doctor. His number one concern was the safety and welfare of his patients. He went from one wounded man to another doing everything possible to help. He assisted his recent appendectomy patient in leaving the ship safely. Many gave him credit for helping them don their life jackets in order to jump into the ocean, in spite of his own injuries.

Lieutenant Robert Carley, our devoted chaplain, gave physical help to numerous men. He gave words of comfort and encouragement to many men who would not survive. He had been an inspiration to his men but now he was especially appreciated in what seemed like a hopeless situation. Exhausted from assisting many to safety, he was rescued from the water by a boat from the destroyer *Morris*. His duties continued aboard ship. He held a service of

11. Rescued

Thanksgiving for the survivors and conducted several burials at sea for the less fortunate.

Captain John Crommelin was a great aviator and leader. He commanded respect by never asking his men to do more than he would do himself. He proved that by becoming an example. He was one of five brothers serving in the Navy and all were Annapolis naval academy graduates. He served as chief of staff of the *Liscome Bay*'s carrier division. Though he was just out of the shower and stark naked, he went from one area to another to help with the rescue and to give directions. With burns and other injuries, he finally jumped into the water, was rescued by the *Hughes* and sent to the hospital.

These were only a few of the men aboard the *Liscome Bay* who lived up to the Navy's tradition of honor, sacrifice and gallant heroism when faced with danger. There were many, many more.

I continued to think and try to process the events. "How could all this tragedy have happened? The *Liscome Bay* and all her excited crew became the victims of a Japanese torpedo in her first major battle! That was not the plan. We were expecting to be together all the way to Tokyo and the end of the war! The battle of Makin was to be our first engagement but certainly not the last encounter with the enemy. Things do not always go according to the plan."

After leaving Hawaii on the way to the United States, we were informed of the safety of the men on the five planes on patrol the day before our ship was sunk. Realizing the danger of the impending storm the pilots requested and were granted permission to land on other carriers. The storm had saved their lives! A possible tragedy had become a blessing.

12

Return to Hawaii

As a guest on board the destroyer *Hughes* and the transport *Leonard Wood*, I had no duties to perform so I spent much time in thought. First and foremost, I gave thanks for being alive and reasonably well-off. Leaving the war behind, we were sailing eastward away from the conflict. The task of leaving the war behind, though, was only wishful thinking. It would follow me even though I did not actually hear the sounds and see the sights; the images were ever-present. My emotions were jumbled—I was full of joy and sadness at the same time. I did not want to think of my buddies' dreams.

On the first night of the journey to Hawaii, two more of the *Liscome Bay* survivors died. I attended their funeral and the burial at sea November 26. The chaplain performed a non-denominational Christian ceremony. The service was sad but inspirational. The message of faith helped give strength and courage to all the survivors who were struggling to recover from the terrible ordeal. Each honored sailor was wrapped in a body bag and draped in a United States flag. Then he was placed on a large plank and allowed to gently slide into the ocean. The ship's bugler played "Taps." The mournful music signified the end of the day for the two men being laid to rest in the waters where they had spent their last days. There were few dry eyes. I felt sick for several hours afterward. I had to talk to myself again. "Come on, Beasley! You're alive for a reason."

I shared a compartment with the burned steward I had helped while we were floating in the water. He was from Virginia and his name was Smith. He was in terrible shape, both from burns and cuts. He was wrapped in gauze from head to toe, with small openings for his eyes, nose and mouth. He screamed in pain day and night and was at times delirious. I had taken his dog-tags from him while still in the water, thinking he might not survive his serious injuries. I would keep them until he could recover or if he did not I would see that they were given to his family. He was in for a long, long battle to get well.

12. Return to Hawaii

Burial at sea for two sailors from the *Liscome Bay*. The service was held on the destroyer *Hughes* rescue ship (Navy Archives).

I often wondered what my family knew of my whereabouts. The military reports to the American people were not always the true facts. If too much was known by the enemy the lives of our men could be in danger. In some cases like Pearl Harbor, the Japanese were not aware of their great success. A bad report could also be detrimental to the morale of our troops as well as to the folks back home. I had heard of Tokyo Rose and her radio propaganda beamed directly at the United States. Her reports on the success of many Japanese battles were often false, and she exaggerated when reporting on the defeats of the United States.

There was no way for me to get in touch with my family while in a battle zone. They knew I left the United States on board the *Liscome Bay* and was a part of the Pacific fleet but just where I was remained a mystery. Had the sinking of the *Liscome Bay* been announced? If it had been reported, they would not know if I survived, was injured or had been killed. I had no way of sending word of my situation.

I stood on the deck looking out over the vast waters, with nothing between me and the horizon but the ocean. What lay ahead? I had heard the phrase "sailing into the wild blue yonder." That was what I was doing, but what was out there in the wild blue yonder for me?

The only unexpected event that I had experienced to compare with my present situation was the death of my grandmother when I was seven years old. We had a good and joyful life together. I had never dreamed it would end as it did. As time passed I realized what a privilege it was to have known and loved her and I found joy in the memories. I still missed her. Will this experience be like that? With the passing of time will I be able to accept it and find joy in life?

However, this was an entirely different set of circumstances. I did not know if I was properly equipped emotionally to handle what I was being forced to accept. My days were filled with visions of my friends and shipmates who were young and looking forward, with hope and confidence, to a great future. Many were now gone. The dedicated men around me, who moaned and cried with pain, were not just a vision but a reality. What will happen to them? Will they even survive? I relived the scene of the bodies being placed on a board and lowered into the water for burial at sea. The words of the chaplain rang in my ears. He spoke of the life hereafter for those men who had given their lives in battle for us—the living.

The nights were even worse than the days. My dreams were flashbacks of the horrors I had witnessed. I saw the lifeless bodies of the bugler and the boatswain killed by the fallen radio antenna and woke with a jerk. The helpless pilots crashing into the water seemed to be a constant nightmare. The view of the dedicated admiral in his work compartment as if on duty kept me from sleeping many nights. Those are only a few of the incidents that continued to disturb me. Again and again I asked myself, how will I be able to experience real joy again or will sadness fill my thoughts? Only time will tell.

During one of my times of meditation, I was approached by an officer who had the report on my signal gang. I was very anxious to finally know the fate of my buddies until he said his report was not good. He told me only five of the twenty-three signalmen had survived the sinking of the ship. My heart sank.

"Who made it?" I asked. As he began to name the five, I thought of my Alabama friend and his dream.

He said, "They were the five who were on duty and were on the upper deck—you, Andrews, Goss, Umbehagen, and Duff." In total shock, I could

12. Return to Hawaii

not speak. Chills ran from my head to my toes—that could not be! The survivors were the five men Williams told me only two days ago were absent from his wedding party in his dream. I don't know how long I sat there trying to think things out. After awhile I revived and again I said to myself, "Get up, Beasley! You're alive!" and I added, "There must be a reason for me to be here."

There were times, aboard the *Leonard Wood* transport ship, that I wished I had some duty to perform. That would keep my body and mind occupied. The terrible sights and sounds of the injured men continued to bother me throughout the voyage to safety and recuperation. There was no way to escape it.

Every crew member on board the ship was wonderful! The doctors, the chaplain, and all the officers went out of their way to make us as comfortable as possible. The stewards served especially good food and prepared it so the disabled could eat without help. They made us feel worthy of the attention we were given. My official injuries were listed as multiple cuts and bruises, burns, severed toe and foot, three cracked ribs, back injury, ruptured ear drum, and internal injury resulting in coughing up blood. However, I was fine! I could eat, move about, see, hear and talk—I was in great shape.

Over and over again I thought, "I am one of five out of a group of twenty-three to survive—Andrews, Goss, Umbehagen, Duff and me! What about Williams' dream?" I could not comprehend everything that had taken place. Would time help me understand the events? Time was a gift I had that had been taken from so many young men.

13

In the Hospital

On December 2, 1943, I arrived back in Hawaii where I had been only three weeks earlier. It seemed like a lifetime and for some it had been. I, along with the other survivors, was taken to the hospital in Honolulu. There I hunted up my friend Smith, who had the terrible burns all over his body. It was obvious he was doing much better and seemed to be in good spirits. In our general conversation, I asked him, "Do you remember Beasley?" He replied, "No, I don't believe I do."

We continued the conversation by talking about the sinking of the *Liscome Bay*. He seemed surprised to hear the things I was talking about and finally he said, "I don't remember anything about it." I explained a few incidents and told him, "I have your identification tags. I'll leave them here on your nightstand and you can let the nurse put them away for you." He understood what I was saying and replied, "OK, thanks." As I was leaving I said, "Try to remember the name Beasley; that's me. I hope we meet again someday and have a long talk." That was not the time to tell him of the terrible experiences we had shared. I was relieved to know he would be all right. I have tried several times to contact him but was never successful.

While in the hospital in Hawaii I had a number of good and bad experiences that I'll never forget. I enjoy remembering the good things and try to focus on them. However, the bad experiences keep popping into my head.

Soon after we arrived at the hospital we were assigned a space with a bed and a place for a few belongings. We settled into our area in the much overcrowded hospital. Some men were in rooms but most of us were in a hallway or some other small unused space. I was in a ward with more beds than room to put them! Suddenly, we had visitors.

Girls in snow-white Red Cross uniforms came into our ward. They were a welcome sight to see. My first thought was "How clean they are! They are prim and proper and have come to help us." We were still covered with oil and other unsightly stains, with mostly make-shift clothes on. My second

13. In the Hospital

thought was "Everything will be OK now that the Red Cross has arrived." They had a ditty bag for every sailor. Graciously, I said, "Thank you." One sailor across the room did not respond to a girl's announcement of a gift from the Red Cross. She placed it on his nightstand. The boy next to me had his head so bandaged he could not see or hear her. I watched the girls move from one bed to the next and I thought, "I guess their gift is a nice gesture."

I opened my bag and took out each item. My thoughts ran wild but I said nothing. What would a fellow, who had lost his arms, do with a pencil and piece of paper? How could the young man in a coma brush his teeth? What will I do with a comb, I have no hair? Oh, well, the intentions were good, I suppose.

In a few hours, the "sunshine" girls came in again to make an announcement. They were going to help us send a telegram home! The men who were able cheered with delight. I said, "That is truly worthwhile to each and every man here! An act of kindness each one of us will appreciate."

While on board the transport ship that carried us back to Hawaii, we were told some very disturbing news. A report in the newspapers back home told of the sinking of the *Liscome Bay* and the article said there were no survivors. The Navy never released the names of ships or casualties until the next of kin had been notified. However, this event was witnessed by several other ships and the word, as well as a very graphic photograph, was printed before the Navy made the official announcement. The headlines across the United States read, "The *Liscome Bay* sinks—no survivors!" Radio announcers picked up the story and also reported it as a known fact. In the hospital ward we had discussed the matter and wondered how our families were reacting to the false report. How could we get the word home that some of us were still alive, maybe badly injured, but alive?

There was much joy among the shipmates of the *Liscome Bay* when the Red Cross came to our rescue. They were going to help us notify the folks back home of our rescue, hospitalization and impending recovery! As the smiling girls circulated around the other side of the room from me, I saw and heard confusion and crying among the men. I was sure they were so overcome with happiness, their emotions were taking control. Thinking of home, Mama, Daddy and my brothers and sisters, I felt tears come to my eyes. I could envision my family at home huddled in front of the radio listening for any word concerning the *Liscome Bay*.

When a Red Cross helper came to my bed she handed me a form to fill out. I followed directions: wrote my name, the name of the intended receiver,

"Get the hell off this ship!"

their address, then began to read more. There were five statements followed by multiple choice boxes to check. When I finished checking the proper boxes, I realized I had said, "I'm alive—today!" I was somewhat disappointed but I said nothing.

I glanced around the room to see how others responded. I was shocked to see no one was helping those who were not able to fill out the paper themselves. I was contemplating going around the ward to see if I could help anyone, when the real clincher came. A sweet young feminine voice informed me, "That will be two dollars." I looked at her in total astonishment and said, "You mean you are charging me two dollars to send this home?"

Aboard ship I had developed a habit of wearing my money belt around my waist at all times. When I had to leave the ship by rope and jump into the water I had it with me, and then as I shed my clothes I kept on my money belt with my undershorts. On the rescue ship I had taken out the wet money and laid it on the hot deck to dry, then placed it back in the belt and fastened it around my waist. There was all of sixteen dollars! As I reached to take out two dollars, I knew why the men were upset—no one had any money! I felt my face turn red with anger as I listened to the typical Navy language throughout the ward. I took out all the money, threw it at the smiling girl and in a very loud voice hollered, "Use this to pay for as many of the men's telegrams as it will cover!" She took all the money and left.

Later I learned a few of the survivors had been able to report to the pay officer for a small allowance. Those in the hospital had not had a chance to do that and did not have a dime to their name. I was truly angry beyond words. I had not even felt this kind of anger for my enemies. They were supposed to be cruel and mean. They were doing a damn good job of hurting us—they sank our ship! But the Red Cross is not supposed to be cruel; they are supposed to be helpful.

I could not erase the thoughts from my mind. How could anyone from the United States look a desperate sailor in the eye and say to him, "I can't tell your wife, or parents, you are not dead because you can't pay me two dollars?" After this unsettling experience, when a clean, well-dressed, paid, smiling Red Cross aide asked if I needed anything, I asked her, "What will it cost me?" I realized many were not on a do-good mission but were enjoying a Hawaiian vacation.

I have a completely different perspective of the USO helpers. On many occasions the USO gave me assistance for free, with love and best wishes. They also went out of their way to entertain us in some of our most depressing times. My hat goes off to them!

13. In the Hospital

While I was on the ship *Hughes*, James Roosevelt, son of President Roosevelt, paid a visit to the *Liscome Bay* survivors. He was a Marine who was stationed at Makin Island one year before. He had been second in command with a group called the 2nd Raider Battalion. He was returning with the Navy as an observer and a consultant as we invaded Makin. When he learned of the *Liscome Bay* tragedy he made a special effort to visit each survivor. His warm handshake and calm but sincere comments helped lift our spirits. He was very understanding but realistic and concerned.

The hospital in Hawaii helped to save many lives of men aboard the *Liscome Bay* after it sank. Some would not have made it back to the United States. However, it was a depressing place also. I knew when I saw a covered body being carried out on a stretcher someone didn't make it. Day and night there were cries for help, loud screams of pain and constant moaning from those struggling to stay alive. I knew I never wanted to be a doctor but truly respected the dedicated ones who worked many hours every day to help us.

I was well enough to be allowed to wander around outside on the hospital grounds in the sunshine. I really enjoyed being outdoors and walking in the fresh air on the beautiful Hawaiian Islands. I was a lucky guy! As I sat on a bench and fed bread crumbs to the birds, I could feel the great lifting of my spirit—and I needed that. Thinking of the last few days, the terrible ordeal I had gone through and now the beauty of my surroundings, I felt like I had been to hell and was now in heaven.

One day, after spending much of the afternoon outside in the sun and sea breeze, I returned to my ward in the hospital to find it empty. A nurse came running toward me in a panic, "Oh, Beasley, I forgot about you not being here! Everybody has been taken to the dock to board a ship for California." I hurriedly grabbed my few possessions and ran out of the hospital. The bus was gone completely out of sight. I spied a mail truck headed in the right direction and jumped in front of the moving vehicle to make the driver stop, which he did with a jolt. The MP driving the jeep said, "Sailor, you can't ride the mail truck!" My response was "Oh, yes I can!" While climbing into the truck, I told them my sad story of getting left behind. They decided I was not crazy and made fast headway to the dock. When I arrived at the loading dock, the last sailor had boarded the ship and the crew was ready to lift the gang plank. I jumped on in one big leap as everybody watched in surprise. I made it!

I surely did not laugh at the time but looking back I can't help but chuckle. What a sight I must have been. Picture this: a half-running, half-

"Get the hell off this ship!"

hopping young sailor with bandages all over his body, scabs on his head where his hair should have been, wearing size forty undershorts tied with a string around his size twenty-eight waist, flopping in size eleven overshoes held on with rubber bands, and now the proud owner of a split-tail hospital gown! That was me. As nice as Hawaii was, this ship headed for the coast of California was not leaving me behind!

14

Recovery

The last week had been eventful and full of uncertainty, to say the least. I had obviously been in a daze from the time my ship was hit, through climbing aboard the *Leonard Wood* on November 25 and until I was taken to the hospital in Honolulu. When I left solid ground in Hawaii and hobbled aboard the SS *Saratoga* on December 5, I had a sense of relief, with the war far to the west of me I was heading east toward the United States. I was glad to be on an aircraft carrier again, this time headed for California for "treatment and disposition," as stated in my official records.

The crew aboard the *Saratoga* wanted to give us a supply of clothes but the store was soon depleted of anything of my size. However, I was given a very large pair of dungarees which I graciously accepted. By this time I was used to having to hold my clothes on with a rope to keep them from falling down to my ankles. I appreciated having a pair of pants and not having to go around in my underwear.

We were on the water for five days, sailing at top speed, and headed for San Francisco. We encountered some very rough weather with waves crashing over the sides of the ship. With no escort vessels accompanying us, we made the journey alone through the dangerous storms common to the Pacific Ocean. The weather was not our enemy and we felt more comfortable in a storm than in the company of the Japanese. In reality we were leaving the war far behind us—but not in our minds.

The *Saratoga* was crowded with men from the *Liscome Bay* being taken to a naval hospital to recover from their ordeal. No one complained about the conditions. Everyone knew we would be cared for in the best possible way and each one would be treated with respect and care. All were thankful to be going home to the United States. We were well fed, doctored, and made to feel welcome in spite of our physical and/or mental condition. Most crew members aboard the *Saratoga* had been in serious battles and understood our situation.

"Get the hell off this ship!"

The aircraft carrier *Saratoga* taking *Liscome Bay* survivors to a hospital in California from Hawaii.

    The crew of the *Liscome Bay* and the crew of the *Saratoga* had much in common besides being aircraft carriers. The *Saratoga* had experienced her share of serious skirmishes. Both crews had learned an important fact: war is not glamorous! And the fight is not about fame, power or fortune but about country, freedom and family. There is a deep and lasting feeling of honor and respect for all our fellow servicemen and especially the fallen.

    I felt at home on the aircraft carrier. Even though it was much larger than the *Liscome Bay*, there were many similarities. I had a strange feeling of belonging. I chose to sleep on a cot on the hanger deck, as I had often done on my first ship, instead of being crowded inside where other crew members were located.

    I had spent many nights in a hammock on the deck of the *Liscome Bay* looking at the twinkling stars and identifying the different constellations that were not visible back home. On calm, clear nights the water was silver and sparkled like diamonds in the moonlight. But not all nights were clear; many were rainy and stormy. There could be total darkness, and believe me, a ship

14. Recovery

moving in the blackness, swaying and rolling, can be a frightening experience.

We rode out a fierce typhoon on the way back to the United States. Though it was very strong it did not hold the fear for me as some storms had previously. The actual darkness of the surroundings was not as bad as the darkness many of us felt inside. The clouds of despair and uncertainty hovered over most of the survivors, even in the daytime, but the nights were the hardest to endure. They were long with little or no sleep. There was too much time to think about one report made by another ship sixteen miles away: "We saw the *Liscome Bay* disaster—the whole ship just blew apart!" That seemed like an accurate description of the event to me.

I learned a lot about the *Saratoga* while I was on the way to the West Coast. She had been in the midst of many hard-fought battles and had suffered much damage on several occasions. Each time she received the necessary repairs and was sent back into action. There had been loss of life among the crew members and new personnel were brought on the ship to fill the vacancies. The same was true of the flight crew which consisted of experienced men as well as young first-time airmen. Replacements of planes and men had taken place after each battle. She was a real fighter! The Japanese were well aware of her presence in any battle in which she participated. We, the *Liscome Bay* survivors, respected her and all her crew. Her status in the United States Navy made our situation more tolerable.

While we were still on board the *Saratoga*, I and three other members of my signal gang got together to compare notes about our recent experiences. Our tales of the last ten days were similar yet different. We were happy to be together again, thankful to be alive and rejoicing about going back to the good old United States. Silence fell over us all as one fellow began to tell of an incident that disturbed him. In hesitation and with emotion he said, "I was floating in the water when one fierce explosion took place. I felt like giving up the struggle to survive when blood and small pieces of human flesh began hitting me in the face. The warmth and smell of the falling debris was almost more than I could endure."

We arrived at our destination in California on December 9, and another signalman and I were sent to the same hospital at the Alameda Naval Air Station. Both of us had been "lost" by the Navy, no record of us anywhere! We jokingly said if we had some decent clothes we could walk away and no one would ever know we left. What a strange dilemma—lost!

We knew there must be some information somewhere about Beasley and Andrews. Checking all lists, we discovered we were listed among the dead! Desperately in need of clothes we needed help to prove we were among the living. The base would not issue the clothes to us until they received the proper information that we were alive. After a few days of no help, I said, "Enough is enough!" I told Andrews, "I'm going to sneak out of this hospital and find someone who will listen to us and give us some help."

Andrews quickly said, "Sam, you're going to get in trouble." I looked him squarely in the face and said, "That might be an improvement! Come on now and say you'll go with me."

The very next day, immediately after lunch, we slipped out of the hospital and went outside. We were certainly not dressed like respectable Navy men and we feared someone might report us. In fact we fit the expression "a sight for sore eyes." Again picture me still wearing the large, floppy overshoes held on with rubber bands, very large dungarees with no belt, only a rope tied around my waist to keep my pants from falling to the ground, a dirty split-tail hospital gown and scabs on my head instead of hair. Poor Andrews did not look much better. We had been wearing the same clothes for two weeks!

Once outside the hospital we looked around and down the street we could see a building with a pennant flying. I said very excitedly, "That is where we need to go—come on! That flag means there is a rear admiral in the building."

Andrews pleaded, "Sam, we are heading for trouble," then said, "but let's go!"

We entered by the front door and went down the hall straight for the admiral's office. Two well-armed patrol officers stopped us and I calmly stated, "We're here to see the admiral." After looking us over, both uttered some very strong and threatening comments and we knew it was time to leave.

Andrews said in a cautious tone, "Sam, let's go back to the hospital before we get into serious trouble." It was a fact—we had no identification, no record of us was found, we did not exist. I was determined to get the attention of the right person. But what more could we do? "I'm not giving up this easily, Andrews. I saw a back entrance to the building. We can go in that way."

Back outside, we walked around the building and went in through the back door. We walked down the hall toward the admiral's office, trying desperately to go unnoticed. The noise of my footwear flipping and flopping attracted the attention of two office workers, a yeoman and a young lieutenant. Just as we opened the door to the admiral's outer office both men called the patrol and the same two officers appeared. We were so close to our goal! We

14. Recovery

began shouting an explanation of why we were there. Just as the patrol officers began dragging us out of the office, the admiral stepped out of his inner office and addressed the shore patrol, "What is going on here?" The patrol chief began to explain but I quickly interrupted, telling my side of the story. We were shouting, each of us trying to be heard over the other. The admiral stood very still and listened. When there was a pause in the yelling match, he spoke quietly, "You two men come into my office."

I thought, "At last someone is going to listen to our story." Andrews and I both said, "Yes, sir!"

After the admiral asked us to sit down, he listened attentively while we explained our situation. We told him how frustrating it had been just to get someone's attention. We had been wearing these same clothes (such as they were) for about two weeks and needed someone to help us. As the admiral sat silently in front of us for what seemed like minutes, we felt like he believed we were telling him the truth. Our appearance was our proof—we needed help! If he did not believe our story, he could send us to the brig or, even worse, send us to the mental hospital ward.

Finally, he picked up a pen and wrote something on a piece of paper. He called the shore patrol in. "Take these two men to the PX in your jeep, then go on to the hospital and see to it that each *Liscome Bay* survivor is issued a full complement of clothing, bed gear, toilet articles and all other basic issue equipment."

Then he turned to us, handed me the note he had written and in a quiet, emotional voice (not common to a commanding admiral) said, "As for you two men, take this note to the storekeeper and I am sure he will issue you a full complement of your needs." We joyfully sprang to attention with "Yes, sir! Thank you, Sir!"

We followed the chief, whose attitude had taken a turn in our favor, climbed in his jeep and smiled all the way to the PX. It took about an hour to get all our equipment. We were issued a sea bag filled to the top with all our precious items. It did not take us long to get to the hospital and get dressed like true sailors. How proud we were of our efforts and our new clothes! I have wished many times I had learned the name of the helpful understanding admiral. By the way, I still have my sea bag, after sixty-plus years!

15

Home for Christmas

After staying in the hospital for a few days, I received a sealed envelope which contained my new orders. Also in the envelope was enough money for a train trip home. This was the first money I had seen since I gave the Red Cross my sixteen dollars in Hawaii. I was being granted a thirty-day leave called "a survivor's leave" to go home for a visit. When the leave was over I was to report to Portland, Oregon, for active duty with an outgoing unit that was stationed there. I wasted no time. I packed all my newly-issued possessions and headed to the train station.

I chose to take the southern route to North Carolina, so I could go through Alabama where my friend's family lived. I knew I would not stop but I just wanted to pass in the general area of William's dream. I had no problem getting a ticket for the very next train headed east.

As soon as I boarded and settled down, I found the trip was relaxing and very enjoyable. I saw a lot of desert with few, if any, trees. It was the same scenery through California, Arizona and New Mexico. It looked just like the pictures I had seen of the southwest and was very fascinating. I liked the landscape better as we got into Texas because it looked a little more familiar. I wondered how big some of the farms and ranches were as we rode through the farming country. We seemed to travel an hour through only one ranch with cattle by the thousands! I'm sure the ranch must have covered hundreds and hundreds of acres, unlike our small farms back home.

I wondered how many days it would take to get to North Carolina but that really did not matter. This was uninterrupted time to get my thoughts together. We rode through Texas and more Texas. Not only is everything big in Texas, Texas itself is big!

This was a great time to reflect again on the past year and all the events of which I had been a part. I smiled as I recalled December 15, 1942, when I took my first long ride on the way to boot camp at the Great Lakes Naval Training Station. It had been one year and three days ago. What a busy year

15. Home for Christmas

and again I thought, "I was only eighteen!" I was so young, just a boy, but now I'm nineteen and a man. One matures rapidly in times of war and conflict. In some ways the year seemed short and in other ways it felt like a lifetime. For some of my friends it had ended their lifetime.

Back to my recollections: Boot camp was a time for learning and really a very pleasant experience. Then I went to Idaho for the training to become a signalman. That was one of my very best memories. Both schools helped me to prepare for the future I was destined to face and I know it was worth the time and effort involved. I remember how excited I was to finally get on the *Liscome Bay* and begin the journey to the South Pacific—and war! Only one day before my nineteenth birthday all hell broke loose!

Now, on board a clickity-clack train headed home, I was wondering, "Was I just lucky to have come through the terrible tragedy alive, or do I have some special purpose for being here? Realistically, all odds had been against me being one of the five signalmen out of twenty-three to make it to safety and in reasonably good shape. Whatever the cause or reason, I'm happy to be here."

There were many stops along the way. I ate on the train or bought a snack or a meal at a train station. In New Orleans I had to catch a different train so I spent one night there in a hotel. The food in New Orleans was good but flavored slightly different. The stop gave me a nice break in the long trip from the West Coast all the way to the East Coast. As we again began rolling out into the country side, I relaxed and enjoyed the scenery. The sights were new to me but very pretty. Though I was alone, there were many travelers who were friendly, so I did not feel lonesome.

When we traveled through the Gulf States, I knew I was almost home as I gazed out the window at familiar trees. For the past year, with the exception of Washington and Oregon, if there were any trees at all, I had not seen pretty ones like ours in North Carolina. Even at Christmas there is greenery in the South and that was a welcome sight. Everything seemed to be alive!

When we crossed the Mississippi state line and entered Alabama, I thought of Williams. He had been a special friend and such a great fellow. I read the name of each town as we passed through one and then another small community. I thought of his parents and his girlfriend. He always carried her photo in his pocket and frequently took it out to show to me. Chuck and I had been very good friends, and when he received a letter from home he wanted me to read it. I read the encouraging letters from his parents, and usually his mother had a message for me. From time to time she sent home-

"Get the hell off this ship!"

made cookies and she knew how much I enjoyed them. I did not read the letters from his girlfriend but smilingly he read excerpts to me. He enjoyed thinking of going home to his family and to his father's farm which would one day be his. He declared Alabama was next to heaven.

I had a feeling of guilt because I knew he had so much to look forward to and had a plan for his future. I was still trying to put some meaning into my life and find my way. Now he had lost it all and I had everything. That was not fair, but it was reality.

I could not help thinking of the dream Williams had the day before the sinking of the *Liscome Bay*. It was uppermost in my thoughts. How could that be? Only the five signalmen who missed his party survived—all those who attended perished. I did not understand but I knew it to be a fact. "I am in the state of Alabama on my way home, sad and happy at the same time." I also thought of Umbehagen's dream. So far the Grim Reaper had not been successful in his warning to me and Pete but the war was not over!

My train arrived in Raleigh, where I caught a Greyhound bus to Winston-Salem and on to Mt. Airy. It was Christmas Eve and all seemed to be well with me as I climbed down the steps of the bus with my sea bag. I looked around and I did not see anyone I knew; in fact, there were very few people at the bus station. I got a cab, gave the driver the address of my home while wondering how everyone would react to me. We did not have a phone so I could not prepare them for the great event of my return. What would this homecoming be like? I could not picture it in my mind. The cab ride home seemed long when actually it took about fifteen minutes.

I walked up the steps, across the porch and opened the door to the living room. One of my sisters took one look at me and ran away hollering, "It's Claude!" Everybody in the family came running toward me, crying and screaming. They almost knocked me off my feet. Mama spoke the first words with a question, "You're not dead?"

Surprised, I said, "Why would you think I was dead? I sent you a telegram from Hawaii saying I was in the hospital but not hurt too badly." She looked at me and asked, "You sent a telegram? We never received it and all the news reports said there were no survivors." I convinced them I was not a ghost. What happened to my two-dollar telegram?

As it was Christmas Eve, Mama had a big meal already prepared. Together for the first time in more than a year, the whole family sat down for a good home-cooked meal. What a time for rejoicing! Mama had made a delicious dressing to have with the turkey, sweet potatoes, and I don't remem-

15. Home for Christmas

ber what else she had prepared. I truly felt at home. Mama, Daddy, my three brothers and three sisters sat at the dining table all talking at once. How thankful I was. However, in the back of my mind I was remembering my friends who would never have a chance at a moment like this.

I tried to tell of the good events that had taken place rather than dwell on the bad events of the last twelve months. I had many happy times I could share with them. Trying to change the focus of conversation from me to other topics, I inquired about relatives, friends and happenings in Mt. Airy. During our happy conversation, we were interrupted by a knock at the door. Daddy left the dinner table and opened the door. There stood the Western Union delivery man with my telegram from Hawaii sent December 9!

This Christmas was very special and still lingers in my memory as an exceptionally happy occasion. Most of my leave time I spent with immediate and extended family but I also found time to meet with a few high school friends. There were many girl classmates but most of the fellows were away in military service. My thirty-day leave passed in a hurry! When it came time to pack up and get on my way back to my Navy duty, I was rather anxious to get on with the business I had volunteered to do. I was grateful to be physically able to return to active duty and do my part in helping to bring the terrible war to a close.

My thirty-day leave lasted from December 18 to January 17, 1944. The freedom from duties, responsibilities and planned schedules was invigorating and good for my spirits but for some strange reason I missed the orders and rigid activities I had learned to respect. I began thinking of my orders to report to Portland, Oregon, by January 17. I left Mr. Airy, again riding the train, in ample time to be present and ready for my next duty, whatever it might be.

I spent several days on the train heading across the country to the far northwest. The views from the window of the fast-moving train were spectacular! I saw miles and miles of the Great Plains, the high Rocky Mountains and then the breathtaking forestland of Washington. There were brief stops along the way for a break from the riding. Almost every town in which we stopped there was a welcoming party from the USO to greet the servicemen. We seldom had to buy food or drink with these great people standing there waiting for us when the train stopped. They served the best donuts and coffee I ever tasted. Their positive attitude made me feel I was appreciated and involved in a worthwhile task.

Sometimes the temperature outside was below freezing but the train was

"Get the hell off this ship!"

warm and comfortable. Though I was traveling alone to my destination, I met many friendly people. It was easy to strike up a conversation with a fellow traveler. Civilians were generally curious but kind when asking questions about my naval experiences, so I never had to talk much about myself. My new uniform gave the impression I had recently joined the service so I usually just told where I had trained. The conversation with other military personnel was mostly giving my name, hometown or state and where I was heading and general chit-chat.

The constant sound and rhythm of the clacking of the wheels on the rails made my mind wander back again to the events of the past year. A new idea came to mind. "What was I thinking during the explosions and the sinking of my ship, the *Liscome Bay*?" That question had not entered my mind before. I could not remember what I was thinking. In fact, I don't even remember thinking! I told myself, "The serious and extensive training I had received guided my actions. I had been drilled to number one, do my job; number two, look after my fellow sailors; and number three, save my life! If I had been thinking rather than reacting, I'm not sure I could have stepped over dead bodies, walked through blood, endured the cries of pain and witnessed the injuries of my shipmates. How and why did I not give up in despair? What was I feeling? Nothing! There was no time to feel, only time for action." To my instructors, I say, "Thank you!" I sincerely give them the credit for me being alive today.

The Navy has a long-standing tradition of courage and heroism. The crew of the *Liscome Bay* demonstrated the true Navy spirit of honor and sacrifice. I will forever be proud to have been a member of that great crew!

16

Guam

After riding the train for several days, I was glad to arrive at my destination in the northwestern part of the United States—beautiful Portland, Oregon! I was ready to start in what I felt was a new beginning in the Navy. All the old days seemed like a dream except that the Navy was my life now. I knew I was bound for active duty and as a trained signalman I knew that was not in an office somewhere in the States. Many *Liscome Bay* survivors were being assigned to a home base, a hospital ship, or some other safe, inactive job. I was thankful I had been declared physically and mentally fit to go back to where all the action was taking place.

My new assignment was on an attack transport ship that was docked in Portland named the USS *Alpine*. At the end of my rehabilitation leave I received a promotion from Seaman First Class to Signal Man Third Class and was scheduled for some more training to serve on this type of ship. For five days, I trained in recognition school, followed by two days of firefighters school. I then went to signal school review for six days and after successfully completing these courses I was ready to serve aboard the *Alpine*.

During the time of my training I took full advantage of the opportunity to do some sightseeing in the area with my new buddies, who were also anxious to get out and see the town.

We requested, and were granted, leave a number of times and found numerous places of interest. I had always heard of Portland as the city of roses, but in January we did not see them in bloom. Not only was the city pretty, the people were exceptionally nice to us. It was a great place to be stationed.

The USS *Alpine* APA-92 was built in California as a ship for civilian use and named for a county in California. The Navy acquired the ship in September of 1943, and sent it to Portland to be converted to a Navy vessel. Many changes were needed to meet Navy specifications. Under the command of Lieutenant Commander George G. K. Reilly, the *Alpine* was officially commissioned on April 22, 1944. It was ready for duty and so was the crew!

"Get the hell off this ship!"

The time of the commissioning ceremony had been set and announced. When we heard the call "All hands on deck!" the crew, dressed in full Navy uniforms, stood at attention to participate in the impressive ceremony. This was the second time I had experienced a ship's commissioning. What an exciting time for all aboard! The war was moving along at a hot and heavy pace, and I knew our military was making progress and recovering from the shock of the attack on Pearl Harbor. However, I could not help but think, "I hope the fate of the *Alpine* is not the same as that of the *Liscome Bay!*"

After taking on ammunition, provisions and supplies, a very proud and excited crew rejoiced when the *Alpine* left the dock at Portland in early May 1944. We sailed down the beautiful Columbia River to the open sea. While in route to San Diego, we had a variety of strenuous, around-the-clock exercises, and arrived there on May 13. These training exercises continued for several days with many of the crew unhappy, thinking we were only wasting

The transport ship *Alpine*, Jim's second ship and new assignment, ready to join the Pacific fleet.

16. Guam

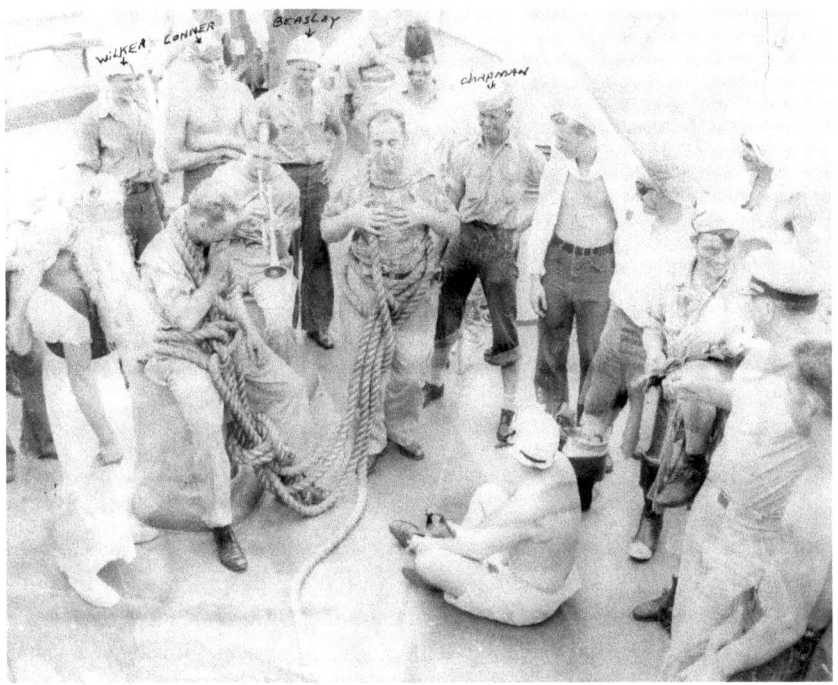

The *Alpine* crew celebrating the crossing of the 180th meridian.

time. I remembered I felt the same way only a few months ago. I had learned a lot about the importance of training and welcomed the time we had to practice and to become acquainted with the ship and each other. In all situations, but especially in time of war, practice makes perfect!

Upon completion of a thorough shakedown in the San Diego area, the *Alpine* left for Pearl Harbor on June 19 and arrived on June 25. Without delay the personnel and equipment of the 77th Army Division began loading onto the transport. With more than fourteen hundred troops and all their supplies, our ship left Hawaii sailing southwest toward its destination. We were taking troops to the island of Guam in the Marianna island group. This invasion was planned to retake Guam from the Japanese and we would also serve as a support vessel during the landing of the Army troops. On June 28, the *Alpine* attached to Transport Division 38 in a designed formation before sailing from Hawaii on June 30 toward Guam.

Spain claimed the island of Guam before the United States took it into their possession. Then Japan invaded it and took it from the United States.

"Get the hell off this ship!"

Now we were determined to retake it as we moved forward on our island hopping effort toward the Japanese mainland.

In an award ceremony on July 4, 1944, I was awarded the Purple Heart for wounds received when the *Liscome Bay* was sunk. I hoped others who survived the tragedy were also being recognized wherever they might be. I was proud to receive the honor.

July 5, the *Alpine* and her crew crossed the 180th meridian. We had the traditional party to initiate the pollywogs. I could understand their excitement but I was not as enthused as I expected to be. I guess I had become a more serious-minded person as a result of my experiences. I was the old sailor called a shellback and had the privilege of giving commands to the pollywogs. I observed the activities with restrained pleasure. Since we were on our way to perform a specific task our time to celebrate was limited.

By July 9, we had arrived at the island of Eniwetok, along with all the other transport ships loaded with Army troops. We had one more very important exercise to practice: the debarkation of troops and supplies. This practice lasted about a week. Back at Eniwetok we replenished all needed supplies and set off for Guam on July 17. It had taken a long time to prepare for the invasion, but everything needed to happen like clockwork in order to be successful in our mission to reclaim Guam.

After sailing for four days as a part of the large Pacific fleet, we reached the Marianna Islands and the west coast of Guam. We arrived at night and all was dark except we could see in the distance gun flashes from our ships. They were bombarding the island in preparation for the landing of the Army. With the light from the constant shelling, we could see the outline of the hills on Guam. Heavy smoke and bright flames rose high into the hills beyond the shore from these explosions. There could not be many Japanese left in the area being targeted by our many fighting ships! July 21 was D–Day for Guam.

The battle raged and even though we were eight or ten miles from shore, the *Alpine* shook all over! Vibrations from the big guns on our sister ships were felt from stem to stern. We slowly moved toward shore as some of our attacking forces moved in closer to the beach. With the help of planes from our carriers, the invasion of Guam was underway. Many of our men were killed or injured by enemy gunfire while trying to reach the beach. Each time an enemy blast was seen on the island, a ship or plane of ours knocked out the exposed location of the Japanese, who had hidden in caves and man-made tunnels. Without the constant help from support ships an invasion would have been impossible.

16. Guam

We watched as the pounding continued all day long. Then about sunset we moved closer to shore and the troops aboard the *Alpine* were called to hit the beach. After most of the men had left the ship, the cargo was off-loaded onto small craft that seemed to appear from nowhere out of the darkness. This activity continued for most of the night. The coral reef along the shoreline made the landing for both men and equipment move slowly. To prevent the enemy from leaving their hiding places and attacking our troops as they arrived on the beach, the bombardment from our ships and planes continued to hit the interior of the island until daylight.

I watched the shells explode in mid-air high up in the sky, and saw the bright flares from our aircraft. I heard, as well as felt, the depth charges released by our destroyers. The enemy knew we were present with one goal in mind. After our first encounter with the enemy, we stayed in the area for six days. Each day and night was a repeat of the previous one. We did not suffer any casualties among the crew on the *Alpine* but there were many among the landing troops. Even after all the troops and equipment had left the ship we stayed just beyond the enemy's reach and remained as a support ship when needed. As we blasted away at the island, we were able to see and hear the raging battle with both sides showing determination to be victorious. That honor came to the United States.

The *Alpine* won its first battle star after six days and nights of very intense fighting before the United States could declare victory at Guam. Our mission was successfully accomplished and each crew member on the *Alpine* was proud of his efforts.

17

Leyte Island

The Guam engagement had been much safer than my last assignment, the battle of Makin on the *Liscome Bay*. After our duties on Guam were completed, we headed back to Hawaii by way of Eniwetok where we arrived on July 27, 1944. From there we sailed to Pearl Harbor, docking on August 7. While repairs were made and the ship was inspected the crew had a few weeks to revitalize body, mind and spirit. We enjoyed the break from battle and headed ashore for some typical Hawaiian recreation. The weeks passed too quickly.

Sometimes mail was delivered to the ship. When in port we received mail covering a much longer period of time. Every sailor hoped to hear his name at mail call and know someone was thinking of him. Most of us had a card or letter and maybe a photo from back home when we returned to Hawaii. I felt sad for those who received nothing. Usually someone shared a message with his buddy. Occasionally a mom sent homemade goodies which were shared and quickly eaten.

I usually had a note from Daddy or someone in the family but the letters were so closely censured it did not tell me much. Anything pertaining to the war was blacked out. I had been promoted to Signalman 2c from Signalman 3c and the increase in rank also increased my pay. When I entered the Navy I had requested to have a large portion of my pay sent home. I knew I had little need for money aboard ship. In Hawaii I received a letter from Mama telling me about the increased amount sent to her and all was being deposited in the bank for my college tuition when I came home.

The next assignment for the *Alpine* was to carry troops from Pearl Harbor to the Philippine Islands for the invasion of Leyte. Before we left Hawaii, we participated in another training exercise off the coast of Maui. We needed to practice amphibious landings with more than fourteen hundred soldiers. We got underway from Pearl Harbor on September 5. We stopped at Eniwetok again and spent three days there loading the ship with supplies. After making

17. Leyte Island

Jim Murphy (left) and Gerald Goss on duty on the *Alpine*.

another stop on the island of Manus, we joined an extremely large task force on October 3. All the final preparations for an invasion were completed and the armada of ships left Manus on October 14.

Manus is an island close to New Guinea in the Admiralty Islands. We had recaptured the islands from the Japanese and were using them as a supply base. There were about eight hundred troops on board the *Alpine* as we headed to Leyte in the southern part of the Philippines. We had been told this would be similar to the Guam invasion but on a much larger scale. The rumor was circulating that the Japanese were expecting us to strike at this location but not so soon. We wanted to surprise the enemy.

We reached the landing destination on October 20 and began unloading troops and supplies immediately. We worked feverishly all day under heavy fire from the Japanese. There was no doubt we were in the thick of an important and decisive battle. I was not aware of the enormous size of our armada of ships at the time, but was concentrating on my job on the *Alpine*. Here, unlike Guam, we suffered some casualties. The intermittent air strikes did not stop us but did slow down the landing. Even though we were some distance from the island, we could see and hear constant bombardment from our battleships. Sand and dust was flying through the air. Copper-colored smoke rose above the rocky shore. The troops had a very difficult time reaching land.

Thinking back over this first landing on Leyte and the battle there, I remember that just as we entered Leyte Gulf, I saw a Japanese plane head for

"Get the hell off this ship!"

a ship in the convoy. I said, "He must be having problems with his plane." Soon I learned it was an intentional effort to dive his plane directly onto an aircraft carrier to destroy the ship. That was my first encounter with a deliberate attempt at suicide by a pilot, or a "kamakazi" attack by the Japanese, but it would not be the last! This pilot was unsuccessful as our gunfire shot him out of the sky before he completed his mission.

All the while we were sending wave after wave of troops in landing craft onto the beachhead of Leyte. Trying to stop our invasion, the Japanese bombers were flying over and dropping bombs on the transport ships. It hindered our efforts greatly and many men were killed or wounded in the unrelenting attack. The process of debarkation was delayed but not stopped. The crew of the *Alpine* shifted back and forth from battle station to unloading equipment then back to battle station. At twilight, all our ships were ordered to make a smoke screen, engulfing the whole harbor, but we continued unloading in spite of the poor visibility. We could hear our ships bombarding the enemy on the island and at times saw flares or exploding shells light up the sky. The flashing lights enabled us to see our extremely large convoy spread out in the gulf.

A group of natives, who had survived the Japanese takeover of the island and had helped us fight against our common enemy, were brought aboard the *Alpine* for medical treatment. Some were in very poor condition but were bandaged up, given clean clothes, and returned to the shore. By their gestures and by the tone of their voices we knew they were expressing gratitude for our help.

The following morning we were still trying to unload amid alarms of impending air attacks. A Japanese bomber was shot down near our ship, barely missing us as it fell into the water. There was also much activity and confusion on the beach causing further delays in unloading men and supplies. An invasion of this magnitude requires many tanks and other heavy ground equipment which is difficult to get off the ship but invaluable to the invading troops.

The task was completed about dusk and a smoke screen was again spread over the area. The *Alpine* was ordered to get underway immediately and move out as the Japanese were closing in. The gulf was crowded with our many nearby ships. Along with the smoke screen, fog began to move in. Fog signals sounded from all directions and suddenly a ship would appear in front of us, much too close for comfort. In addition to these obstacles, there were Philippine trading vessels in the harbor using us as a protective shield. We managed

17. Leyte Island

somehow to feel our way out of the gulf and we stayed close to the coast in order to avoid detection. Again I was happy and relieved when we got far away and were leaving the sights and sounds of battle behind. I preferred to sail in the open water. The *Alpine* earned another battle star.

The United States was holding its ground in the Pacific area; in fact, we were gaining over the Japanese. The kamikaze pilots proved Japan was concerned about our military power.

Much later I learned more details of the landing of troops on Leyte. The Japanese knew, even though they did not admit it, this was basically their last stand before defeat. Halsey's Third Fleet was the strongest in the world. More than seven hundred United States ships were involved in the Leyte Gulf invasion and thousands of American troops readied to go ashore. In desperation the Japanese had created their "special attack units" hoping the daring kamikaze fliers could use their suicide attacks to save the Japanese empire. All of our ships were targets but especially the aircraft carriers and the transport ships. We, with only a few guns, were limited in our ability to defend ourselves.

By some reports, the battle of Leyte Gulf was labeled the greatest naval engagement ever fought. Others described it as the most dramatic battle of World War II. The area of water our fleet covered was twice the size of the state of Texas. The number of ships involved has never been equaled and all possible elements of war were involved, from submarines under the water to airplanes in the air! Our strategy of surprise by striking earlier than expected was in our favor. The Japanese put forth everything possible in an effort to resist our forward movement. The fierce fighting lasted several days. The *Alpine* had completed her job and had left before the heaviest fighting took place. We headed back for more invasion troops and would return.

While the major battles continued in Leyte Gulf, we were assigned to take the wounded to the hospital in Hollandia, New Guinea, on our route to pick up more soldiers. This time we loaded fuel and provisions and sailed to port Biak in the Schouten Islands. On November 14, after loading the Headquarters Squadron of the Fifth Army Air Force, we made a return trip to Leyte Gulf, but further north than before. Our troops disembarked the *Alpine* on November 18.

The previous battle of Leyte (October 20) was where General Douglas MacArthur fulfilled his promise to the Philippine people after he had told them in March, "I shall return!" And so he did. We were close enough on the *Alpine* to witness his return. We could not see him personally but saw the activity unfold and felt the happy excitement of the event. Everyone was rejoicing—except the Japanese!

What would we face in this second battle of Leyte? The first battle of Leyte had been more difficult than our encounter on Guam. I asked myself, "Will each new conflict become harder and more dangerous than the previous one?"

After several encounters in battle aboard the *Alpine* I learned more about the role each type of ship played in the effort to complete a successful invasion. The duties of the crew on a transport ship are different from the duties of the crew on an aircraft carrier. They have the same concerns of safety, for danger is real and always present. However, when we had troops on board, our main thought was to deliver these men safely to the point of invasion.

I became aware of the trust placed in the aircraft carrier by other ships. They were truly the lifesavers of the men being placed into battle when they landed on an island. They were present to supply the air patrol before, during and after every invasion. Each type of vessel in the convoy had its special part to play in the success of the outcome of a battle.

As I watched men from the Army and the Marines making their landing on the beach, I was pleased with myself for choosing to join the Navy. The invaders seemed to have a slim chance of surviving. Many men were mowed down as soon as they hit the beach or even while still in the water. War is terrible!

18

Second Battle of Leyte

Battles were being fought throughout the islands of the Pacific Ocean, not just in our location of the Philippine Islands. All branches of the United States military, Army, Navy, Marines and Coast Guard, participated. At that time each branch had its own air force, and without the airplanes we would have had a very difficult task of winning back any of the islands. There was little rest for any of us. When we were called upon to do a particular job, and each and every one put forth his best effort to fulfill his responsibility. There were no shirkers among us!

The United States had learned just how well prepared the Japanese had been to pursue their mission of conquest. They were making plans long before they attacked Pearl Harbor. Time is a valuable asset in war and we lagged pitifully behind, but with sheer determination we were catching up on the home front as well as on the battleground. Factories were putting out equipment in record time with around-the-clock operation. We showed our determination to prove we had the power to defeat Japan and in no uncertain terms!

On our second trip to Leyte, the enemy was waiting for us. While our troops were off-loading the *Alpine*, three Japanese bombers and three fighter planes greeted us! As the bombers unloaded their bombs on our ships, anti-aircraft fired from all directions at the enemy planes. The gun crew on the *Alpine* sent one suicide plane and its pilot into the water. Another plane passed directly over the signal bridge where I was standing and the pilot turned the nose of the plane quickly downward and headed straight for the *Alpine*. Just before hitting the ship the plane burst into flames and hit us with a terrific explosion. The plane hit the side of the ship where a three-man crew on board a small landing craft were waiting to load and haul troops to shore on the island. The vessel and all the crew were blown to splinters!

The kamikaze plane left an ugly hole in the *Alpine*, and the plane quickly burst into flames. Debris, including bits of metal, littered our ship as the plane burned and disintegrated. Also particles from our ship were scattered over the deck. Everything was blazing hot! The crew worked feverishly to extinguish the flame and after about thirty minutes all was under control.

Five men on the *Alpine* had been killed and twelve men injured. As the ship burned, I remember thinking, "Is it over for the *Alpine*? Is this a repeat of the *Liscome Bay*?" That thought lasted about one second before I told myself, "Not so fast, Beasley!"

I have great praise and respect for the fire and rescue parties. Training and practice do pay off and the quick response from the crew members saved the *Alpine*. When the flames were quieted and the debris were removed, the unloading of men and equipment continued as if nothing had happened. Occasionally our work was interrupted by an alarm and we were called to man battle stations.

The task group commander sent a message of praise and congratulations to the crew of the *Alpine*. We were very highly praised for our exceptionally good timing and the excellent work we had accomplished. A job well done! The message was encouraging to us, but the joy was overshadowed by the loss of our shipmates.

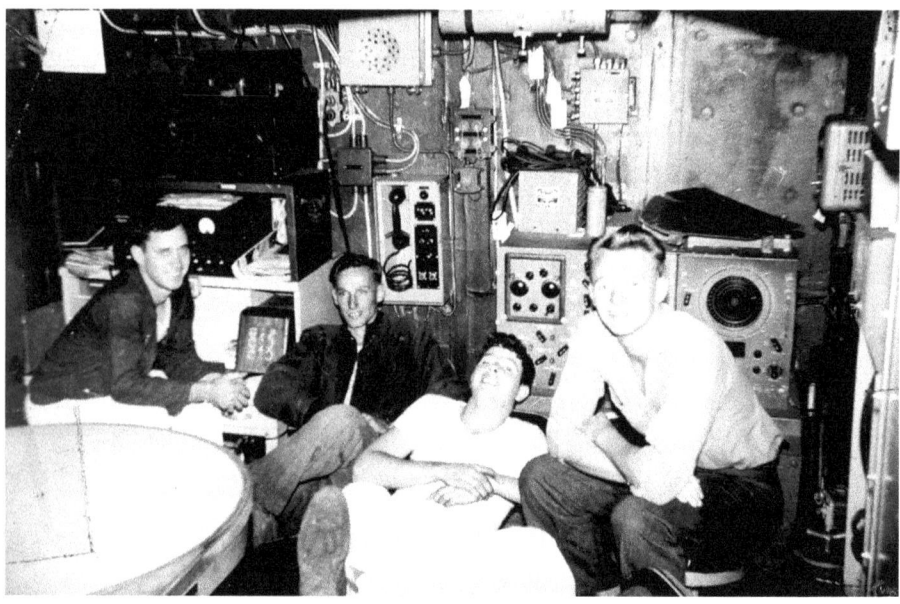

Shipmates relaxing in the communication room.

18. Second Battle of Leyte

When we left Leyte, we headed to Manus in the Admiralty Islands not far from New Guinea. The *Alpine* needed hull repairs suffered when the kamikaze plane hit the ship. These were to be makeshift repairs that would be sufficient for us to return to action. The efficiency of the repair men amazed me. Regardless of the damage, the repair crewmen were capable and had the equipment to make our ship sea-worthy again.

While we were anchored in the harbor for several rather idle days, November 24, 1944, rolled around. My mind was fixed on the events that had taken place one year ago. I had thought about the sinking of the *Liscome Bay* every day, however there was something about it being the one-year anniversary that seemed to take hold of my thoughts. First, I thought of my friends who had their lives cut short by the tragedy. Second, I wondered what had become of the other survivors. I also thought of my last birthday, when I had turned nineteen years old on a rescue ship in a condition I now know was shock. I began to tell myself, "That was 1943, this is 1944 and tomorrow will be my birthday and I will be twenty years old—November 25, 1944! In those two years I lived an eventful life. What is next? There is much more of life, even if the youthful lad of eighteen has become a man of twenty. Get on with it, Beasley!" I always had a habit of talking to myself.

19

Luzon

We remained in the harbor at New Guinea for about a week before heading back into battle. On December 1, we had fifteen hundred Army troops and equipment on board going to the Philippine Islands, but this time we were going to the northern part, to Lingayen Gulf on the island of Luzon. Our troops were trained in jungle warfare and would be facing fierce Japanese fighters who had dug themselves into the deep jungle in their desperate attempt to hold on to their position. Since this would be new fighting tactics for us we participated in an exercise in tactical and antiaircraft gunnery skills to better prepare all aboard for the landing that was ahead of us.

Christmas of 1944 came and went. There was some effort to remember this important time of year but our work was urgent and we had to keep our minds on the job before us.

The ship's cooks served a traditional Christmas dinner with limitations. The chaplain held an open Christmas service for those who could attend. Christmas mail arrived to brighten the day but mostly we were busy with routine preparations for another invasion.

By the end of December, after replenishing all our supplies, we were on our way to Luzon. As a transport ship we were always loading and unloading troops and their equipment! Not being a fighting ship we hoped there would be little conflict but that was not what usually happened. We joined the Seventh Fleet when we arrived in the Philippine Islands area. We sailed around Manila Bay and Clark Field which was still being held by the enemy. We tried to keep our distance from shore but sometimes we were too close for comfort as we made our way to our intended destination.

For four days and nights we were under constant alerts for enemy air attacks. Each day seemed to get a little more active and dangerous. On January 7, 1945, a lone kamikaze plane flew directly over us with three of our fighters following close behind. The Japanese plane was brought down and it landed in the water only feet from the *Alpine*.

19. Luzon

The most fierce dog fight I witnessed took place on January 8, when four enemy planes we called "Zekes" approached the task force. Fighter planes from our carriers engaged them and we watched as the air battle progressed. After a bomb was dropped with no damage done, one Japanese plane was sent into the water, and soon another was splashed as smoke came from the tail of the plane. The other two tried to get away but it was useless. They were taken down also.

In about an hour, two more Japanese planes came into view flying high, trying to avoid gunfire from several ships. One plane dived into an escort carrier. Though the carrier was heavily damaged their crew put out the fires and saved the ship. That was not the end; only moments later two more Japanese planes came over. All ships opened fire, literally lighting up the sky. One plane headed straight for the *Alpine*, but our gun crews pounded the plane. It went out of control, burst into flame and splashed into the water.

Johnson proud of the *Alpine*, ship number 92.

The days we spent at Lingayen Gulf were eventful to say the least. The enemy seemed desperate to stop our advancement and prevent a successful invasion. Warning messages were exchanged between our ships about swimmers with deadly explosives tied to their backs trying to reach the ships. Reports came to us that suicide boats were slipping in among us at night and there were kamikaze planes constantly flying overhead. A few of the planes were successful in hitting their targets but most ended up going into the water engulfed in fire. Japanese bombers were dropping missiles, occasionally finding their target. I don't know how anyone, the Japanese or the Americans, came out of the battle alive, but I did! However, many of our men were not as fortunate as I was.

At twilight on January 8, all the transport ships were ordered to move out of the bay to open waters where we could move around and not be direct

"Get the hell off this ship!"

targets for the suicide attacks. The swap of two Japanese pilots and his plane in exchange for a United States carrier with planes and crew or a transport ship carrying hundreds of men was not an acceptable swap for us. The *Alpine* cruised through the night to return in the morning to her anchorage. At dusk on January 9, another group of Japanese planes came in and they scored a direct hit on one of our transport ships. A terrible tragedy—there were many men lost. But the job of unloading troops and equipment on the *Alpine* continued amid the fire of the defenders of the island. Upon completion of our mission in Lingayen Gulf, the *Alpine* headed back to prepare for another assignment.

Each engagement was similar but very different in many ways. I was amazed how our quartermasters planned for our needs. They never knew how long we would be on a mission and what the circumstances might be. Seldom did they miscalculate any supplies. Not only did they prepare for the ship's crew but for the troops we had with us. Occasionally we delivered food and equipment to the natives who were on the island assisting us. Thanks to the Quartermaster Corps!

While aboard ship, both the *Liscome Bay* and the *Alpine*, I was fascinated with the process of refueling. We always left port with a full supply, but on a mission far from any fueling supply station, we often found ourselves running low and that could be a disaster! From out of nowhere a big tanker ship came to our rescue. When the water was calm there was no problem attaching a large hose from the supply ship to our ship. However, in most situations, rolling waves made one ship ride high and one sink low in the water. I never witnessed a collision but I have seen a time when I looked straight down on the ship bringing us the fuel and vice versa. It was scary to think of two of our own ships having a serious accident when trying to keep everything moving properly. The accuracy of the procedure was remarkable. On the *Liscome Bay* I also enjoyed watching planes being refueled in mid-air. It was amazing to me to see how the connections were made while both planes were moving through the air.

Only a week later, the 38th Infantry of the Army boarded the *Alpine* for the trip to Subic Bay, also on the island of Luzon. We engaged in an exercise of amphibious training before lowering the boats of troops on Luzon. We luckily met little resistance and were there for only two days, January 29 and 30, 1945. We delivered several loads of troops for the deadly battles to retake the Philippine Islands from the Japanese.

The ground battles on the islands had been terrible. When the Army or

19. Luzon

Marines landed they faced snipers everywhere. The fight was man to man. A Japanese soldier might suddenly appear from nowhere with a gun, and a quick decision had to be made—either me or you! I did not envy the invaders and wondered if we were taking our fellow troops into a death trap. Maybe we were but we all had a job to do and no one failed to follow orders when called upon.

Battles like we were involved in brought to mind the lesson our instructors taught us. "Watch for the enemy—get him before he gets you!" A slogan of the Army was "Mow 'em down!" But I was puzzled by the statement "Fight a fair fight." What is a fair fight in war?

We continued to be attacked by subs under the water and by planes overhead. Death and injury were facts of life. Every time we reached port new recruits came on as replacements for casualties among our crew.

The battle for control of the Philippines was now history and the United States claimed victory. Other countries were doing their share of fighting in several battles in the Philippines. I remember seeing an Australian transport loaded with troops prepared for an invasion. We rejoiced!

20

Time for Reflection

For most of the month of February 1945, the *Alpine* acted as a support ship in the Philippine Islands for smaller craft in the area. Our ship was being checked over for known needed repairs and also for routine repairs. This break was good for all the crew. We were pretty well stressed out with the schedule we had followed, not to mention the continuous battles of which we had been a part.

Now was a good time to view the war as spectators and not participators. Where had we been and where were we going? That was something we had not had time to think about. We were happy to learn the fact that it was apparent to the United States and to Japan that we were gaining more of a foothold in the Pacific. We cheered each time the United States took control of another island on the road to Tokyo! We learned more about the difficulties the Army and Marines had faced in their invasions. Not only had they dealt with heat, rough beaches and the Japanese, they were also dealing with jungle thick forest, malaria and, on some islands, head-hunters!

I felt as if I had been rewarded by being in the Philippine conflict because it was so vitally important to us—and Japan. These islands would be our most strategic base as we moved forward. We had been told that after our assignment of being the landing craft repair boat was completed we would be ready to go back into active battle again.

The *Alpine* had been in many battles but we knew there were many more to come; the war was far from over! We knew our next engagement would be the transfer of troops and support for the invasion of Okinawa in the Ryukyu Islands. The United States was successfully following the plan of island hopping on the road to Tokyo. But where was Okinawa?

My friend Dale Wilker, also a *Liscome Bay* survivor, was in the navigation unit on the *Alpine*, and he showed me a map of all the Islands in the Pacific Ocean. He helped me trace my journey from the United States to Hawaii and

20. Time for Reflection

on beyond toward Asia, and more especially Japan. I could see clearly the plan the military officials had devised in chasing the Japanese back to their homeland.

We looked at several of the groups of islands where battles had been fought before I joined the Navy. I remembered soon after the attack on Pearl Harbor, General Douglas MacArthur was forced out of the Philippine Islands. The famous USS *Lexington* had been sunk in the terrible battle of the Coral Sea. Then the battle of Midway took place with the worse naval defeat for the Japanese in centuries! Our victory at Midway gave the United States the morale booster and confidence all Americans were looking for. On a map it is very obvious how Midway got its name. In the middle of nowhere, it is midway between North America and Asia.

At this point, I recalled how everyone back home in Mt. Airy had talked about the landing of the Marines on Guadalcanal in the southern part of the Solomon Islands. The jungle on the island was as much of an enemy as the Japanese. For about six months, the savage fighting was described by radio reporters. Sometimes our Marines seemed to be gaining ground, then the Japanese would get back in control! History now records the Guadalcanal battle as the longest and bloodiest campaign in the whole Pacific war.

The *Alpine* signal crew in Manila Harbor, 1945. Back row, left to right: Click, Beasley, Weiss, Goss, Watsabrugh, Williams, Johnson and Moyer. Front row, left to right: Murphy, Cozard, Polson, Chapman, Vote and Forrest.

"Get the hell off this ship!"

When I became a part of the Navy the Japanese still held Midway, but abandoned the island in February 1943. This had been the first step on the planned road to Tokyo and the defeat of Japan. Most of the world cheered us on!

Still looking at the map, Dale and I followed the islands westward and discussed the area the Japanese had taken and the area they were planning to conquer. I remembered hearing of the battle of the Bismarck Sea but could not recall what took place. Looking at the Aleutian Islands, a part of Alaska, I thought about our forces landing there to protect them from being taken over by the Japanese. Japan was really getting close to the United States!

Not long before I had my first encounter with a battle, I learned the United States was sending troops to the most northern island of the Solomon Islands, at Bougainville. Aboard ship we heard it was a severe battle and many lives were lost. It lasted for many long months.

Now my friend and I found names on the map that had a personal meaning to us. Tarawa and Makin, in the Gilbert Islands, were battles we truly understood. Here we paused a moment to reflect on our *Liscome Bay* experience at Makin. It seemed far back in the past but still like yesterday.

Next were the Marshall Islands, with Kwajalein a stepping stone to Tokyo. We missed that important battle due to our time of recuperation back in the States. Eniwetok, also in the Marshall Islands, became an important port for the United States after retaking it from Japan. While on the *Alpine* we were sent there many times for supplies en route to another island invasion. The Mariana Islands, which were even closer to Japan, was the next target. Admiral Chester Nimitz put together an armada of more than five hundred ships under the command of Admiral Raymond Spruance to go against the Japanese-held islands of Saipan and Guam. Here is where we came back into the picture for real. What a large group of ships. We had sailed right along with the best of the United States Navy!

I looked at the tiny islands of the Marianas and wondered how those specks on the map could be so important to cause such a terrible fight for their possession. Saipan was a very difficult struggle of twenty-five days while I knew firsthand the fight for Guam was not an easy one. Tinian was also taken from the Japanese and became a valuable stopping place for our western advancement.

My eyes shifted toward Japan and I could see we were now in striking distance of the home islands with our bombers. We had gotten close enough to send B-29 Superfortress planes to Japan and bring them back to a base

20. Time for Reflection

controlled by the United States, unlike Jimmie Doolittle's first raid on Tokyo, when the pilots had to land in China.

I feel chills when I think of the Doolittle raid in 1942 when the all volunteer pilots left the U.S. carrier *Hornet* with thirteen B-25 bombers headed for Tokyo, knowing full well they could not carry enough fuel to return, and would be at the mercy of their situation. They could only hope for a successful landing in China or in the water to be picked up by somebody. Seventy-one of eighty men came out alive but nine did not return. What an impact it had on the people back home. In Japan it was a disgrace to "lose face" because of weakness or defeat and we were causing them problems!

We continued to look on the map at more islands, especially the Philippine Islands. We had been in and out of Leyte and Luzon several times taking troops for the large invasion. The goal was to destroy much of the Japanese stronghold in the Pacific. Looking north on the map we saw Okinawa! It was a small island in a little group called the Ryukyu Islands and was almost on Japan's doorstep. "Okinawa! Here we come with the great United States Navy!" Dale commented, "It sounds like you are bragging." I replied, "You bet I am!"

After we had studied and discussed the map, the full picture became clearer to both of us. We agreed that the Japanese made a bad mistake when they decided to bomb Pearl Harbor! The United States had not been totally asleep because we were making long-range plans, if and when the war did come to us. When it was on our doorstep we acted like a swarm of bees—mad and determined to sting the enemy hard. We were on our way to give them their just rewards. We would keep moving on, headed straight for Tokyo!

Soon the *Alpine* would be leaving her present position on Leyte, after serving for about six weeks as the temporary repair ship for landing craft used to unload merchant ships in the harbor. Our job could be considered a working vacation. No one had time for a real vacation but we needed a change. Though we worked hard there was more time for rest and relaxation than when in battle, not to mention the lack of stress and mental anguish.

During our diversion from conflict, the Marines were having a terrible time on the isolated Island of Iwo Jima, the closest to Japan the U.S. had been up to this point. The Marines had landed there on February 19, 1945, and by February 23 they had raised the United States flag on Mt. Suribachi, only seven hundred fifty miles from Tokyo. But the Island was not fully secured until March 26. During this time our big B-29 bombers were constantly making raids on Japan. The report claimed that sixteen square miles of Tokyo

"Get the hell off this ship!"

was destroyed and one hundred thousand Japanese had been killed! We also suffered great loses in the battle for control of Iwo Jima, but we were getting closer to our goal.

The map study had sparked my desire to get on with my job. Knowing we had many allies with the same objective in mind made it even more urgent to move forward as quickly as possible. I wanted to be right in the thick of the action! I was ready to be on the move with great expectations of defeating Japan—soon!

21

Okinawa

The time had come for the *Alpine* to leave its repair duty in the Philippines and move back into the active part of the war. We took on a full capacity of troops and practiced landing exercises for about a week before sailing for Okinawa in the Ryukyu Islands.

Still in the dark but just before dawn, we, along with many other ships, arrived at our destination. We were prepared and ready for a crucial and intense battle. Combat troops were lowered into boats which were waiting in the water to carry the men to shore. Every man was scurrying around doing his specific duty in silence with speed and efficiency. A few Japanese planes flew overhead and our anti-aircraft blasted away, splashing the planes one by one into the water.

But all did not go well on this Easter Sunday morning of April 1, 1945. As the troops were leaving the ship on amphibious craft headed for shore one boat quickly returned to the ship. What a horrible sight! Just before reaching the beach a shell had burst above the small boat and all aboard were either killed or severely wounded. A coxswain from another boat had boarded the damaged vessel and guided it back to the *Alpine*. Our doctor and medics worked diligently most of the day helping the few who survived the blast. Those who were less fortunate were properly cared for by other crew members. This was not a good start to a very important mission after our time away from the war. We had to adjust quickly to our return to duty and danger.

The aircraft carriers, destroyers and other support vessels did a super job of trying to protect the transport ships and their small landing craft that carried the men ashore. However, there could be casualties when things went wrong in an invasion. It was impossible for every plan to go as intended.

The crew aboard the *Alpine* had lots of firearms and ammunition to unload as well as the large items like tanks, trucks, jeeps and amphibious tractors which had to be hoisted over the side of the ship into the landing craft. It was not an easy job but an important one.

"Get the hell off this ship!"

When daylight faded and darkness approached, the *Alpine* weighed anchor to move to another less obvious location. Suddenly, from out of nowhere, three planes appeared! Someone shouted, "There come those damn planes with the red circle!" Our guns blasted and tracers streaked through the sky. All aboard the ship knew instantly what could happen next. Our ship still had only temporary plates in its side after the suicide plane hit us in the Philippine Islands. We watched each plane. One headed straight for the battleship *West Virginia* and another exploded mid-air. In spite of the blasting guns, the third plane circled and dived toward the *Alpine*! It flew directly over me. I'm not sure whether I saw it or just imagined the sight, but the pilot was wearing a white scarf and laughing as he flew over my head! The plane hit with enough force to pierce the steel deck. The whole ship shook and flames rose high into the sky. Several men were severely burned and many others were tossed overboard. It was a terrible blow to the ship and crew.

Well-trained firefighters quickly poured water into the large hole in the ship. Any moment tons of explosives still on board could ignite. When the fire worsened, the officer in command gave the order to flood the compartments. For two long hours the crew stood on the side of the flaming pit with water hoses trying desperately to contain the blaze. It looked like a hopeless situation but no one was ready to give up the fight to save the *Alpine*. I remember telling myself, "Don't even think about the ship sinking!"

A salvage boat came upon the scene and we were encouraged that the ship could be saved. High-powered streams of water were poured into the fire coming up out of the large hole. For two more hours the men from both ships fought the blaze, knowing at any time they could be blown to Kingdom come! Finally only smoldering debris remained. I said to myself, "I'm still here and the ship is floating." I was glad I had not heard someone yell, "Abandon ship!" I knew the situation could have been much worse.

I had been assigned the specific job of destroying, by throwing overboard, all books of secret documents in case of a disaster. I had gathered the heavy books which were coated with lead to make them sink to the bottom when someone shouted, "The fire is under control and the ship will not sink!" Very happily I returned the books to their proper location.

After some searching, the suicide plane was located in one of the refrigerator spaces. It had penetrated three decks. The body of the pilot was nearby in a pile of twisted metal. Several of the ship's crew were injured but there were no deaths among us. Total casualties among the invasion troops on board were sixteen killed and nineteen injured. I tried to understand the

21. Okinawa

The author (right) working signal lights in 1944 on the *Alpine*.

Japanese culture of human sacrifice, but in desperation I guessed one life was not considered important.

After six days of continuing air attacks and some temporary repairs, the *Alpine* left the combat area on April 6 and headed back to the United States. The gallant ship was in no condition to engage in another battle.

We were aware that the USS *Alpine* had performed her duty well in this event, the last planned island invasion before the big one: Japan itself. Okinawa was a formidable task for the United States to conquer from the Japanese. However we had prepared well for the difficult task. The United States 5th Fleet had a force of fifteen hundred ships! There were twelve hundred supply and transport ships carrying one hundred and eighty thousand assault troops. After the *Alpine* left the battle zone, fierce fighting continued on land and sea for many weeks. The organized Japanese resistance ended on June 21, 1945, but surprise attacks continued from hideouts and caves for many more months.

The *Alpine* left Okinawa for the United States. She was not finished with her duties in the war in the Pacific, only being repaired for further battles. We said she was on an earned rehabilitation leave. She had now earned her fourth battle star.

"Get the hell off this ship!"

The USS *Alpine* with side damage after a kamikaze attack by a Japanese plane.

I recall looking at the huge swells on the water and wondering where the next invasion plans would take us when we returned to duty with a fully-repaired ship. Would it be another step toward Japan or possibly one of Japan's many islands?

As we moved slowly but surely through the water, a radio crew member received a very sad message. He announced to everyone, "The President has died!" The great man known as FDR had been loved and respected by so many American citizens and he had just been elected to a fourth term as president. We, like everyone back home, were in shock. Now what? I recalled the stern words by President Franklin Delano Roosevelt to the nation, "It will be a long, tough road to Tokyo."

Harry S. Truman was immediately sworn in on April 12, 1945, as president of the United States. We now had a new commander-in-chief. How would the country fare under his leadership? And how would the war progress? Little was known about his abilities and his ideas of moving forward. Many were fearful of what his decisions might be concerning the war. Aboard ship the topic was seriously discussed but we knew time alone would tell how he would act or react.

22

In Seattle

Our journey to Seattle, Washington, for repairs was long, slow and dangerous. We made a short scheduled stop at Saipan and another one at Pearl Harbor. Hawaii was a most welcome sight to see for all aboard but we were anxious to get back to the United States.

As we sailed through the usually beautiful and peaceful waters of the Pacific Ocean we encountered waves we had not seen before. We were approaching an enormous storm which we could not avoid. A typhoon in this area is something not to be taken lightly. It could be extremely dangerous but there was only one choice—ride it out!

Many of the officers had experienced bad typhoons before, but for most of us, it was a learning lesson, a lesson we hoped never to repeat! The ship swayed and rocked violently as high waves crashed over the sides. Our lives were in great danger and there was not a thing we could do but watch and pray! In battle when there was danger we fired the guns and had at least a fighting chance, but not here. Would a storm be our downfall?

In amazement we stood and watched from a normally safe location on the ship as the navigation crew steered the ship at an angle to the waves. The high powerful waves were capable of breaking the ship into pieces if met head on. With a crippled ship we were especially at the mercy of the storm. Direction was forgotten and we went where the wind and water took us. We were sometimes on top of waves and sometimes under the waves. That was a wild ride!

The storm seemed to last forever but it was only for a couple of days. We came out into the usual sunshine and gentle breeze with thankful and happy hearts. We had won again!

However, we still had the challenge of the crippled ship. It had a list so bad some items aboard slid from place to place with the slightest turn in direction and the storm had made matters worse. We were constantly making some adjustments because of the mechanical and structural damage. We were

"Get the hell off this ship!"

Celebration in Seattle, June 22, 1945. Sailors left to right: Goss, Murphy, Umbehagen, Beasley and Vote.

encouraged that since the ship had ridden out the bad storm in one piece, she could take us to Seattle! The *Alpine* was a survivor and we would be too, for now.

We traveled the width of the Pacific Ocean at half speed, with the limping *Alpine* slowly sailing into dry dock at the naval station in Seattle on April 30, 1945. What a trip we had made but all were safe and sound in the good old U.S. of A!

The crew members were ready to celebrate after their many adventures and were delighted to be in the great city of Seattle. We had been there before and knew how everyone welcomed the sailors to the area. The USO was always ready to help in time of need or to furnish great entertainment for the weary servicemen. We graciously accepted all their generosity.

Lots of events happened while we were out of action in Seattle. The whole United States and her allies celebrated "Victory in Europe" on May 8. Though we were still very much involved in war in the Pacific, we welcomed V-E Day and the defeat of Hitler. That also meant we would have undivided help on our fighting front and the defeat of Japan would come sooner—the sooner the better!

22. In Seattle

On June 21 all aboard the *Alpine* personally celebrated the victory of the battle for Okinawa! We had been a part of the initial struggle for this important stronghold and appreciated the men who had continued to fight for months to secure the island for the United States.

In San Francisco, on June 26, an event took place which was of great importance to the whole world. Representatives from fifty nations met and signed the World Security Charter which established the United Nations. The meeting became the topic of conversation on and off the ship. The document was long overdue as a great instrument for peace. However, one sailor expressed what each of us had in the back of our minds: "I'm all for the idea, but it may not help me. Soon I'll be on my way to fight in Japan and chances are I'll not return home." No one responded.

We followed with great interest the progress of General Douglas MacArthur in the Philippine Islands, a place we had become attached to after spending much time on three different missions there. By July 4, the announcement came of total liberation of the entire group of islands. Another cause for celebration!

Though I was back in the United States, I knew the war for me was far from over. Being a signalman I was privy to many plans as they were being made. I had received messages directed to the admiral about secrets of the

The hospital ship *Hope*.

"Get the hell off this ship!"

war that were not publicly announced. At times I was asked to relay plans of action from one person in authority to another. I was fully aware of the next step for us after taking Okinawa. Japan was only a few hundred miles away and would be our next target. We would be hitting the Japanese homeland with all the power the military could put together.

Speaking of sending and receiving messages, I participated in several memorable situations as a signalman. Not all messages were military business. One of the older long-time officers called me to his quarters. He wanted to send a wedding anniversary message to his wife. It was a lovely, romantic message of a few words of endearment. I noticed a slight blush on the face of this firm-speaking, hard-as-nails military man. I gained even more respect for him. I hoped each time the message was relayed the sender honored the privacy of this caring husband for his wife. I also received many personal messages to other officers which I honored with silence.

My friend and former signalman from the *Liscome Bay*, Andrews, was assigned to the hospital ship *Hope* after he recovered from his injuries. On one of our island stops, I saw his ship anchored at the same port. I sent a message asking for him. Andrews and I had a great reunion by Morse code but were unable to meet in person.

On another occasion I saw a ship with a familiar name docked not too far from us. I sent a message and asked if an old high school classmate of mine was aboard. I got an affirmative answer. As we talked we learned both ships were to remain in that location for several days. I was anchored out in the water and he was at the dock but we were able to make arrangements for me to visit his ship and spend the night. We had a great time catching up on our experiences in the Navy. The next morning I looked out at my ship. Plans had changed and the *Alpine* was making preparations to get underway! Somehow, I convinced a sailor to take me in a boat to my ship before it left me behind, AWOL! I never tried that again.

Now I'll continue with my story about our long stay in the port at Seattle. In early May we were placed in dry dock for a very extensive overhaul and full repairs of the damaged ship. We did not know how long it would take before the job was completed. All of us, a shipload of restless sailors, wanted to make good use of our time in port!

This friendly city provided many interesting activities for visiting servicemen. The permanent residents went all out for the sailors who came for a short time and then moved on again to their mission overseas.

The USO in Seattle was one of the most active in the entire country.

22. In Seattle

There were always men and women on duty ready and willing to help with a serviceman's needs, whether it was money, food, directions or friendship. They were prepared to give so much more than coffee and donuts, but they did have a supply of both twenty-four hours a day. At the USO we met local people who invited us into their homes for a visit with their families to share a good home-cooked meal.

I enjoyed top-notch entertainment there many evenings with my buddies when we were on leave from duties aboard ship. This was during the Big Band era and the USO invited well-known swing bands to perform for us. We could eat, drink, talk and dance the night away with a pretty girl!

Most evenings I listened to familiar music from bands I had heard on the radio but on one occasion I was especially impressed with a visiting band's version of "Tennessee Waltz." The leader spoke with such an accent I could hardly understand him but his musicians were very talented and the band had a unique sound. The leader was Lawrence Welk! Later I attended another of his concerts in California. The band was very good and played all types of popular music.

I had an opportunity to see and hear another favorite and popular swing band led by Guy Lombardo. Before I left the Navy I attended many concerts with great band leaders and popular singers performing. I hoped to hear Glenn Miller and I knew he was performing for troops away from home but in the European area. When he was lost in a tragic airplane accident, the news came to us by way of an announcement over the loud speaker.

There were a number of good movie theaters, excellent restaurants and bars throughout Seattle. Most businesses offered discounts to sailors and many advertised free services to all military personnel. I could understand why several of my Navy friends settled in or around Seattle after they left the service.

A disturbing incident happened to me while in Seattle. My fellow signalman and good friend Umbehagan, who had the dream about the Grim Reaper, was going to town to spend the evening with a girl he had met. I was on duty and unable to leave the ship to go with him. He asked if he could borrow my medals and ribbons to wear on his Navy dress suit for the important date. I was happy to grant his request. The evening passed and he did not report back to the ship. I was very concerned, more for his safety than for my medals. Days went by and no word from Pete. We prepared to ship out and still no one had heard from him. We left Seattle for California and after docking there the Navy located him. He had intentionally deserted to be with his new wife! What a shock for all his friends. The Navy tracked him down and arrested him. He was court martialed and sentenced to hard labor. He was given a dishonorable discharge. What a sad story for a fine Navy man and a good friend. I guess it was love at first sight.

23

The Surprise

After almost three months a total patch-up was completed on our ship and we headed out once more to the Pacific war zone. The *Alpine* had not yet finished her work with the great United States fleet! This time we were expecting to prepare for the invasion of the island of Japan.

A refresher training course was scheduled for us along the West Coast from July 21 to July 25. This would tell us if all the changes in structure and equipment were working properly and in good condition as well as giving the new crew members practice in performing their duties. We sailed to Oakland, California, where we loaded supplies and personnel for shipment to Okinawa, which had become a supply depot. It had been secured by the United States only one month before but was already a strategic base for the Navy.

Our new journey from the States began on July 25, 1945. We reached Pearl Harbor on July 31, and after a very brief stay we left Hawaii en route to Eniwetok, arriving there on August 9. All had gone well with the ship and the crew.

Eniwetok is a large atoll in the Marshall Islands. Japan had controlled it but never developed it into an important base. In January of 1944 the United States began to bombard the Island with little Japanese resistance by sea or air. After very slight opposition by the enemy, who were hiding in caves and tunnels, the Marines secured the island with few casualties. It was soon covered with United States military equipment, provisions and troops.

We soon left Eniwetok and got back on course sailing the big and beautiful Pacific Ocean headed westward into the unknown. From the top officer to the lowest seaman on board the *Alpine*, each man was dealing with his future possibilities. The somber attitude was evident throughout the crew. Little was said, but all realized the danger ahead as we went about our daily duties.

We had not actually entered the war zone but messages and announce-

"Get the hell off this ship!"

ments were cautiously restricted and we wondered what might be happening. Even most of the signalmen were not fully informed other than reporting to Okinawa and waiting for a more complete assignment. On August 15 we were on our way to Ulithi, a small island in the Western Caroline Islands. On the *Alpine* were five hundred "first wave" Marines ready for an upcoming invasion. This was to be a minor operation before the big assignment, though it was an important step toward victory over Japan. In our group of ships was the mighty battleship *North Carolina*! What a beautiful ship sailing through the water. I'm sure she looked more beautiful to me because of her name.

We had a surprise and certainly unexpected announcement over the loud speaker. In an excited voice the officer stated, "Cease all fire, hold everything, hostilities have ended!" The good news brought on loud cheers as everyone began to celebrate! Could that be true?

Thoughts rapidly ran through my mind. I assumed the fighting ended because of Major General Curtis LeMay's unending attacks. He had ordered B-29 bombers to hit Japan with fire bombs, which almost destroyed the city of Tokyo. General LeMay had played a big part in the victory over Germany and was now leading strikes on Japan. During the spring and summer he had sent hundreds of big bombers loaded with tons of incendiary bombs on missions to all parts of Japan. They had made strikes on more than sixty of Japan's largest cities. We received one report that stated, "Japan's night sky lights up from fires caused by United States bomb strikes." In the late 1960s I met General LeMay in Raleigh. We lived within several blocks of each other and his children attended the same schools as my children. He was a fine man.

As crew members looked at each other in wonderment we asked, "What had convinced the Japanese to give up the fight after so much hard fighting?" We were told, "The atomic bomb!" An atomic bomb—what is an atomic bomb? In total amazement, I wondered what had been going on that we were not aware of. We were given a simple explanation of an atomic bomb and told the United States had been working on it for months in secrecy.

With much lighter hearts, we continued on toward our destination, arriving at Ulithi on August 18. Instead of thinking about the one million casualties predicted in the invasion of Japan, which would be many of us, we concentrated on a brighter future. I had been thinking, "Will I make it this time or will my good fortune end in Japan?" Now I thought, "Thank you, God, I will get through this war alive!"

While in Ulithi waiting for our next orders we had time for serious thought and discussion. There was much praise for President Truman. He

23. The Surprise

was showing the world he was a man of action and determination. Though he was criticized by many for dropping the devastating bomb and killing so many Japanese, we thought he had saved the lives of just as many Americans. War is never fair but the attackers should be the ones to suffer, not those who were drawn in as defenders. We were happy that we no longer had to look up at the sky searching for the kamikaze planes with the big red circle, diving straight for our ship!

It was September 3 when we received our new instructions. We were to leave the rather lone island of Ulithi, "somewhere in the Pacific," and head for Buckner Bay in the Philippine Islands to join a group called the Amphibious Force of the Pacific Fleet. When we reached our destination we loaded troops and headed directly for Korea with plans to occupy the country.

Aboard the *Alpine* the whole atmosphere had changed. We still performed the same duties but with a feeling of great accomplishment and no fear of attack. We carried many troops destined to be of service to others rather than to kill or be killed. Bad news had turned into good news! "The Rising Sun" was setting fast! There was also great relief for the nations of Asia and the islands in the Pacific Ocean.

The *Alpine* anchored at Jinsen, Korea, on October 16 and unloaded the units of the 6th Infantry Division. What a relief to be hauling passengers without any concern of an enemy! When we finished our task in Korea we went to various ports in China. We made brief stops in Taku, Weihaiwei and Tsingtao to pick up American forces for passage back to the United States. The *Alpine* began its preparation for a joyous but long journey to San Diego, California.

I don't believe I have ever seen people so happy! Most of the sailors and marines had been resigned to the idea of possibly never returning home. They had expected to fight to a long and devastating end. I was among that group. As a signalman I had relayed many invasion messages which were not encouraging as to the outcome and many concerning the difficulty of bringing the war to an end. In fact I was aware our group of ships was to be used as a fake target when we made a landing in Japan. The plan was to send us in the first wave of invaders on the southern part of Japan to attract attention. Meanwhile the main invasion was to happen in another part of the islands. The plan would be a surprise for Japan and a good strategy for the United States but bad news for us personally. What a relief to have this change in plans.

24

The Bomb

After the surprise announcement of the surrender of Japan, we learned more details about the United States dropping the atomic bomb. We were told bits and pieces as the days passed and our immediate mission changed.

The United States had been working in secret for several years on a bomb much more powerful than the ordinary bombs we had been using. The research was extensive and the testing proved satisfactory. When the Japanese flatly refused an offer by the Allies for a plan to bring the war to a close, President Truman decided on a very bold move. He thought we should drop the big bomb on one of Japan's important industrial cities.

The island of Tinian in the Marianas was being used by our B-29 bombers as a home base for raids on Japan. Raids were constantly being carried out from the base and were proving to be damaging and very effective. However, when the Japanese said no to our peace offer another plan needed to be put into action.

Volunteer airmen were screened and a few were chosen for a specific secret and dangerous bombing raid planned by top military personnel. This assignment was described as "a most important job to help end the war." Not one volunteer declined although none were told until the last minute what his job was to be. Little did any one of them know they would go down in history and be known by name throughout the entire world.

By early August all plans had been finalized and the B-29 known as the *Enola Gay* took off from the airfield at Tinian. The pilot was Colonel Paul Tibbits and his bombardier was Major Tom Ferebee from North Carolina. Two other B-29s were sent on the raid to assist with geographic and atmospheric observations and to record and photograph the mission. Captain William Parsons armed the bomb in flight and the other crew members were told just what their mission was to be. There were many concerns before the flight and others along the way, but the goal was successfully accomplished on August 6, 1945.

24. The Bomb

The atomic bomb weighing ten thousand pounds was dropped on Hiroshima. Major Ferebee's aim was perfect. Once one of Japan's most strategic cities for the manufacturing of military supplies was now in ruins! There had never been an explosion of this magnitude made by man. The mushroom cloud rose almost four miles up in the air. There was total devastation for five square miles. Each man in the crew of seven was amazed and concerned. The co-pilot said, "What have we done!"

After this terrible event, with a casualty count of more than seventy thousand, the Japanese leaders remained firm and vowed to continue the fight. President Truman made another bold decision. On August 9, a message was sent to Japan in the form of another atomic bomb, this time directed at the city of Nagasaki. The action brought results.

We had not known about these activities as they were taking place,

Three celebrating sailors. Left to right: Johnson, Koupe and Bailor.

but after the news was out, there was much discussion aboard ship about the dropping of such a destructive weapon. We were all in shock. Was the great war over?

As horrible as the bombing seemed to be, it was better for us than the alternative we faced. In an invasion of Japan, top United States military leaders estimated our casualties would exceed one million servicemen! The American people were told it would be a blood bath. The Japanese civilians were being armed to fight to the death when an invasion came and if necessary they were to use farm and household tools to defend themselves. There was not an estimate of how many Japanese would die in defense of their homeland.

The invasion of Japan by the United States was labeled by the planners

"Get the hell off this ship!"

"Olympia." Besides the loss of life, Olympia would require effort and money that could possibly be beyond our capabilities from halfway around the world.

President Truman believed and had stated that he thought the role of president was to be a good leader. He said, "A leader must make tough decisions," and he had many difficult decisions to make. The choice of dropping the atomic bomb or invading Japan was an extremely tough decision. He knew Emperor Hirohito started the war with the intent of being the all-powerful ruler and he must be stopped at any cost. We must lead the way. Encouraged by our actions many of the nations in the Pacific joined us in the final struggle to defeat our common enemy.

Hirohito stated, "The Americans are so savage I will end the war." On August 10, the Japanese emperor surrendered and the formal army was no more! However, throughout the Pacific Islands many Japanese soldiers engaged in forest, tunnel or cave warfare. Hirohito knew he must announce defeat to his countrymen. On September 2, 1945, the official treaty of unconditional surrender was signed on the battleship *Missouri*, in Tokyo Bay. On the *Alpine* we all cheered and rejoiced. Japan was no longer a threat to us.

25

War Is Over

The many foreign ports we visited were fascinating to me. Of course I had seen pictures of the people and the strange places in Asia in books, but being there was much different. At some ports we did not leave the ship but on most stops we had the privilege of shore leave. We all took advantage of the opportunity to see these unusual far-away places.

While I was in China I just had to ride in a rickshaw! The little man pulling the cart in which I was riding ran all the time! How he endured for hours with only short stops was amazing to me. I bought several items from local traders to bring home for members of my family. Trading was an experience in itself. Not understanding each other's language, we did price dickering with motions. Most dealers were so anxious to have some American money they sold their wares for practically nothing. At that time Chinese money was almost worthless. I traded a few American coins for a large bag filled with Chinese money!

When we completed the first pick-up of troops we left port for San Diego, arriving on November 18 with a ship crowded with anxious war survivors. Our passengers disembarked with joyful hearts and loud cheers! The docks were covered with friends, families and total strangers. All were laughing and crying at the same time. I never saw such a large welcoming group or so much hugging! These heroes had gone from fighters to homecoming veterans.

The ship's crew rejoiced with the happy returnees but we all knew this was a temporary visit for us. Soon we would head back out to the Pacific waters to complete our mission of picking up many young men stranded far from home. After all the general maintenance and needed repairs were completed to the *Alpine* in San Diego, we would be on our way again. For several days we worked hard throughout the day but were usually granted leave for evening activities. San Diego was a great place for a sailor to spend his leisure hours away from his duties.

"Get the hell off this ship!"

A big attraction there was crossing the border into Tijuana, Mexico. Sometimes sailors got out of hand on a fun-filled evening. However, there were usually enough buddies traveling together to keep control of the situation. A street artist asked to paint my portrait. I was delighted to stand for a few minutes while he painted a full-length picture of me in my Navy uniform. When I got back to the ship and proudly displayed my portrait, I learned most of my buddies had a portrait also. I ate at very good restaurants with some of my friends in Tijuana. We had a great time celebrating together!

The month of November was coming to a close and I had many things for which to be thankful. The conflict with the powerful Japanese nation had ended, Thanksgiving was approaching, and I was going to celebrate another birthday! On November 25, 1945, I would be twenty-one years old. The time had passed fast since I entered the military almost three years earlier, but I felt I had aged at least six years. Was I really only eighteen when my life changed so quickly?

We loaded supplies on the ship as we prepared to return to the western Pacific in early December. We were sailing with much lighter hearts and would be in safe waters for our Christmas dinner. It was a well-prepared traditional meal.

The food aboard ship was quite good, especially when not at war. I have great praise for the cooks on both the *Liscome Bay* and the *Alpine*. The stewards were dedicated and very conscientious in serving not only healthy food but good and appetizing meals for everyone. Since we had large refrigerators, meats and fresh fruits and vegetables were on the menu every day. We had learned early

Celebrating the end of the war. Left to right: Doe, Weiss, Beasley and Henslee.

25. War is Over

in our days on the ship one very important lesson. If ice cream was served on a hot metal tray, eat it immediately! When we were docked in the tropics, we had special treats like fresh bananas, pineapples and coconuts. I never got my fill of the fruits and nuts there, even when I went ashore and bought them for snacks.

Our next trip was to Nagoya, Japan, with about two thousand Army occupation troops. After their departure from the ship, we again loaded with Army troops to take back to the United States. We had another Christmas dinner especially for them. The Army troops were happy to be treated to a good, home-cooked meal, many were in tears. Going full blast, we headed back to the United States, docking at Tacoma, Washington, on January 14, 1946.

During the last few months of service I sailed thousands of miles on the blue waters of the Pacific Ocean without the threat of danger from an enemy. The ocean and the islands, and usually the weather, were beautiful beyond description. I enjoyed immensely my Navy experiences in the Far East in late 1945. Seldom was the atomic bomb discussed aboard the *Alpine*. The feeling of being alive and returning home far outweighed the feeling of doubt about our use of the terribly destructive bomb.

In time of war our trips from one port to another were filled with duties of preparation and action with an opportunity for a brief nap. Occasionally we found time to play cards, mostly "nickel poker," for maybe an hour or two. When the conflict ended and we were traveling most of the time, several of us arranged for an ongoing card game. When one player left the game for duty another player took his place. This series of games could last for a week or more! I was lucky and won my share but also lost my share. However, I left the Navy with an extra blue Navy uniform and several other items. I won the very last game we played on board the *Alpine*—our well used set of poker chips! How would I explain to my family how I acquired these things? I had been taught not to gamble. If I could get through a war in good shape surely I could convince my family I had not become a real gambler. I was only playing to pass the time and have fun with friends.

I had many things to talk about and to show when I reached home. The purchased items made in China had been very carefully packed away. I knew everyone would be interested in all the exotic places I had visited and anxious to hear of the many strange customs of people from the Asian continent.

As I traveled back to the United States, I realized with mixed emotions this was the final working voyage for the *Alpine*. She had served her country

"Get the hell off this ship!"

well and had been my home since April 22, 1944, when she was commissioned in Portland, Oregon. That was her whole life as a Naval war vessel and a big part of my life in the Navy—and forever!

A couple of days after leaving Hawaii, I received a message that Captain Reilly wanted me to report to his office. "What have I done?" rushed through my mind. Quickly I made my way to his quarters trying to imagine why he wanted to see me. After I gave him a formal and proper salute, he asked me to be seated. My heart was pounding! He calmly stated he had just completed studying my records and wanted to know if I would like to stay in the Navy. What a relief—I had not committed a crime!

He went on with the interview, praising me for my excellent performance of duty and response during stressful times. He stated I had the qualifications the Navy looked for in their choice of men seeking a career in the military. He added he would recommend me highly for a promotion immediately if I wanted to continue in the Navy. Captain George Kenneth Reilly was not a person you wanted to say no to.

However, I gathered my thoughts and responded, "Captain Reilly, I am greatly honored by your proposal and your comments on my work and character but I cannot accept your offer." He showed little emotion as I continued, "I am going to college on the GI Bill. I have been accepted at N.C. State and have already sent in my $10 to the school to reserve a room." Why I went on with my comments, I don't know, but I said, "Sir, I need to earn a piece of paper saying I have a degree. It takes a long time to get where you are, and with no disrespect to you, I want your job!" Then I paused not knowing what to expect from him.

I saw a surprised expression on his face so I quickly continued. "I admire you and the job you do and it takes a lot of time, effort and experience to get where you are. I need to get on with my schooling." He simply replied, "I respect your decision, but if you ever change your mind, come to see me." I rose from my chair, saluted him and left the office feeling I had completed a job of which my captain and I were both proud. I also felt proud to have given him a complete and firm answer of my intentions for the future. However, somewhere inside I had a feeling of guilt. Had I let my great and respected captain down? He had been my hero for almost two years.

I was making preparations to leave the ship and my friends in Tacoma, but would not be discharged until I reached Norfolk. The *Alpine* was scheduled to make the trip through the Panama Canal to Virginia and most crew members from the Eastern part of the United States planned to stay aboard.

25. War is Over

For some reason I felt the need to leave the ship when it first landed on U.S. soil. I disembarked in Washington and rode across the country on the train. As it turned out it took as long to get to Norfolk on the train as it did by sea!

So many servicemen were returning home the train was terribly overcrowded and made many long stops. The weather was extremely cold and disagreeable that January. The ride was not the relaxing trip like my other train rides had been. I was more drained physically, mentally, and emotionally than I realized at the time. But I reached my destination wondering how I had made the three-and-a-half year naval journey without giving up. I accepted the fact I was totally exhausted and very anxious to be home.

My second ship, the USS *Alpine*, had served as an assault transport for almost two years and I was with her throughout that time. She had performed well under the many difficult situations in battle and treacherous weather conditions. In the Norfolk naval shipyards on April 5, 1946, she was decommissioned and her name struck from the list of Navy ships on duty on May 1, 1946. During that time she had earned five battle stars and a Navy unit commendation for her service as a transport ship in World War II. Every crew member on the *Alpine* was proud to have served aboard the honorable ship!

26

Discharge and Transition

On the long train ride going home, I relaxed as much as possible to get my thoughts in order. The task was a difficult one even though the war was over. Most of the celebrations were also over and the military returnees did not get any special treatment. The train was cold and ill-equipped for all the passengers heading for some Eastern destination. There were a number of delays, from bad weather to operating malfunctions, including an out-of-order heating system. The Rocky Mountains were unusually icy and treacherous. We all complained some but most of the civilians and servicemen tried to be nice and considerate. However, I got stuck with an over-talkative man sitting next to me. He was not only full of questions, he had all the answers! I was glad when he got off at Chicago.

As we passed from state to state I recalled the men I had met from that state. Some were special friends and others just buddies, but all were men with whom I had much in common. Several would not be making the journey back to family. I felt very blessed.

The first evening on the train as the light faded and everyone seemed to be engaged in thought instead of talk, a new idea popped in my head. When I entered the Navy I was taken to special training camps and was taught and coached for months on how to act and react in my new role in life. I spent more than three formative years learning and experiencing an entirely new way of life. Now I was leaving that behind and going back to where I left off—or was I?

As I thought about my situation a strange idea came to mind. The war was hard to erase from my brain. Could I be like the airman being dropped from a plane with a parachute, leaving a known and familiar location and dropping into unfamiliar territory with little guidance? I could fall successfully to the proper spot and do well or I could miss the target and be a failure. I had little training for the new role I would play. The world was quite different

26. Discharge and Transition

in many ways, and not only had the world changed, I had changed since I was eighteen years old! The adjustment would be difficult.

The days passed slowly as the train rolled eastward toward Norfolk, Virginia. I was getting anxious to get on with my life as a civilian. As I climbed down the steps of the train there was a feeling of uncertainty. I was given instructions of where to stay as well as the time and place to report for my formal discharge. When I arrived at the designated office, I was informed I would qualify for compensation for my injuries. I asked, "What do I need to do to receive some financial compensation?" The officer answered, "Go to the hospital for a check-up, take your medical records, stay there and in about three days all the paper work should be completed." I quickly responded, "Three days! Forget it! Give me my honorable discharge so I can be on my way." He very kindly encouraged me to follow through with the paperwork as it would be in my best interest. I wanted out now! I was upset and tired—tired of waiting, tired of confinement, just tired!

I received my honorable discharge from the Personnel Separation Center at Shelton, Virginia, on January 24, 1946, with the rank of SM2c. On the paper Officer Parlee stated, "Does not want to reenlist." I was paid my regular amount of the monthly payment of $83.39. I was also given $14.80 for travel expenses and the usual "mustering out" pay of $100. With cash in hand I went to the Greyhound station and bought a ticket to Winston-Salem and on to Mt. Airy, North Carolina. Sad, happy, anxious and confused, I boarded the bus for home. It seemed like a long trip but it became a short trip as I contemplated my future. I was leaving the Navy behind and beginning a totally new adventure. Was I prepared and ready for what lay ahead?

When I reached the bus station in Mt. Airy, I half-dragged, half-carried my duffle bag with all my worldly possessions packed inside, hailed a cab and gave the driver directions to a home I had never seen. My parents had bought a new house since I had visited them. As I climbed into the vehicle a woman came up to me and enquired, "Claude, what are you doing here?" I recognized a neighbor I had not seen in years and answered, "I'm coming home from the Navy." Her welcoming reply was "Ohhh." There were no bands, no hugs, or any displays of appreciation for me. My new home was on RFD #4. When I arrived there my family happily greeted me with hugs.

Home at last! I had anticipated this event and thought I was ready to get back into the swing of civilian life and just continue where I had left off. It did not exactly work that way. It was hard for my family and friends to understand why I was restless, almost unhappy at times. Nearly every day I experienced a situation that seemed difficult to deal with. Being accustomed to routines and schedules, I found that even making decisions as simple as where, when, and what to eat an unpleasant chore. Little uncertainties in my daily life were confusing. I worked at adjusting and basically all went smoothly. I worked, played and set about making plans for the days ahead. I was thankful to have the privilege of having a future to look forward to!

27

Back Home

My brothers, Clarence and Paul, who had also served in the Navy, had come home. My three sisters and youngest brother were in school and stayed very busy. There were always lots of activities going on in and around the house. Mama had many things to do with a large family to care for and Daddy was still working at the furniture factory. Business was now prosperous so he worked long days and most Saturdays. They were both very happy to have the family back together again!

All of us had changed since I left home four years earlier. My brothers and sisters had grown up, especially the two youngest ones. I certainly knew I had changed. For several months I helped at home as much as I could while making plans to go to college. I visited aunts and uncles as well as other relatives. High school buddies and I spent time together catching up on the events of the past few years. Many of my friends had also been away in military service. We sometimes spoke of our experiences and found similar stories but each one very different in many ways. Some of our special friends did not return home and we visited with their families when possible. The months of leisure passed quickly and the time had come to leave home again. To speak the truth, I had gotten restless and was anxious to get on with my plans.

Rather than going to engineering school at N.C. State in Raleigh, I enrolled at Catawba College, a liberal arts school in Salisbury, North Carolina. I and two of my high school friends from Mt Airy began attending classes in the summer of 1946. Both of them were also veterans using the GI Bill to be able to attend college.

After returning home from the Navy, I worked several part-time jobs and saved enough money to buy clothes and all my necessities before entering Catawba. The GI Bill furnished enough money to pay for tuition, books and other fees associated with my classes. There was an allowance for reasonable lodging and limited food expenses. The money the federal government

"Get the hell off this ship!"

The author and his wife leaving home for their first jobs in 1949—Jim as a high school teacher and basketball coach and Elsie as a seventh-grade teacher in Yadkin County, North Carolina.

awarded me was well spent and greatly appreciated. I also worked in the college maintenance shop for a little extra spending money. On weekends I was a short-order cook at a barbecue restaurant near the college. That was a great job!

My first summer semester was a refresher course and was designed especially for returning veterans. We reviewed high school math and English, but mainly practiced getting our minds and bodies in study mode again. Dormitories, classrooms and all other facilities were overcrowded but I did not mind. After all, I had lived in an extremely limited space for four years. I attended school for twelve months each year for three years and graduated

27. Back Home

in May 1949. I was serious about getting an education to be prepared for a good job and a successful life, however, I wanted to enjoy the journey along the way!

I thought of my college days as a time to be young and free again. I had missed that for four years and I had learned to enjoy some excitement now and then. There was not a lot of adventure in attending classes and sharing simple activities with students four years younger than I was! I tried to do well in my studies and I participated in intramural sports and other activities on campus. For a variety I joined the Blue Masque Club and had a great time working with all phases of dramatics. I signed up for unusual courses like Greek!

I made a lot of new friends at Catawba. Though many were veterans, we seldom talked about our wartime experiences. I do recall one friend telling me about his French class. Most of the students were just out of high school and learning from a book, but he had been stationed in France for a couple of years and had learned to speak the language. With a wink, he said he knew many words the teacher did not know, and could not find in the English/French dictionary!

I joined the Navy Reserve when I was discharged although I vowed that when I left the service I would leave all my memories behind. That was easier said than done! I stayed busy with school, work and play so I had little time to talk or think about my days in the military. Little did I know the Navy was keeping tabs on me. Graduation week I had a surprise visitor—a Navy recruiting officer sent for me to meet him in the veterans administrative office on campus. I was offered the rank of 1st Class Petty Officer to reenlist. What a shock! I had not expected that to happen. I was getting married in two weeks and moving to another area in North Carolina to teach and coach high school sports. I declined the offer but suggested he keep in touch with me.

After graduating from Catawba with a certification to teach, I married and began teaching in Yadkin County, North Carolina. I had met my wife, Elsie Lowe, in college and we both were lucky to get teaching jobs in the same county. However, we taught there for only one year. I still had about sixteen months credit on my GI Bill and wanted to take advantage of a good opportunity to get a master's degree in education. I enrolled at Peabody College in Nashville, Tennessee, and completed a course that qualified me to be a school administrator. We moved back to North Carolina and continued working in the field of education until retirement. We added three daughters to our family and had a good but very busy life. I taught and also coached several sports teams before moving into the position of principal and later I became an assistant superintendent.

While in Nashville, we participated in a number of activities and enjoyed our leisurely days with few responsibilities. One day after an intramural basketball game, while still in the shower, I heard someone call for Beasley. I wrapped a towel around me and came out of the shower to find a Navy recruiting officer standing in front of me! I was still in the Navy Reserve and being followed everywhere I went. Again, I was offered a tempting position in the active Navy.

Once more I declined, explaining I had a job waiting for me and in three months I would be a father. Walking away from what I had accomplished back in civilian life did not seem like the wise thing to do. We left Nashville in the summer of 1951 and moved to Newland, North Carolina, where I taught in the high school. After I became the principal we remained there for thirteen years. We lived a normal, busy life with three girls, jobs, and a home to keep us occupied.

Once again, this time in Newland, I had a surprise visit—a Navy recruiting officer! We were reasonably settled, content and becoming a part of the community. Though the unpleasant events of my service days lingered in my mind I had tried to dwell on the good times I had while in the Navy. So when I was confronted in the cold, dreary month of February with an opportunity to be an officer in the Navy, I thought of Hawaii and California! Elsie and I discussed the situation at home and weighed all the pros and cons. For a week we contemplated the possibility of me accepting the tempting offer. I think the uncertainty in the world helped us decide we did not want to give up our lifestyle and opportunities for the possibility of being in a war situation.

28

Navy Friends

I did not forget my friends with whom I had shared so many good and bad times. After arriving home I contacted several fellows and we exchanged phone calls, letters and even visits through the years. From time to time I would lose touch with someone but many of us continued to stay in touch in one way or another. I still find great joy in thinking of our experiences together.

Harry Weiss was a signalman on the *Alpine*. He was from New Jersey and came aboard the ship in Hawaii as a replacement. We got along exceptionally well from the beginning. He was a good guy and loved to smoke a pipe. His mother kept him supplied with Prince Albert tobacco. Many of us smoked so it was not a problem except in close quarters like our signal shack. One day I called him aside and said, "George [his Navy nickname], don't light your pipe in this small signal shack; it is hard to breathe in here." He didn't respond at the time but later in the next watch duty he struck a match to the pipe he had just filled with tobacco from his big Prince Albert can and began to smoke. A terrible odor came out of the pipe and the smoke made every one cough. George began to get dizzy and had to leave the room. Those of us who were in the area smiled as we looked at each other. Finely chopped rubber bands added to his sweet-smelling tobacco got better results than a few words! He and I laughed about that for sixty years.

Harry was the first friend I visited after we left the Navy. While in college I went to his home for a weekend. His family welcomed me as if they had always known me. We had a great time together. Many years later, he and his wife Betty came to Raleigh to visit me and Elsie, and we went to see them in Rochester, New York. We enjoyed getting together and continued to correspond. After both of us retired, they came to Emerald Isle, North Carolina, for a short visit and liked it so well they stayed a week and found a home in Beaufort! A year later they had the house on the waterfront ready to move into and lived out their life near the ocean. We continued to visit each other regularly. "George" and I entertained our wives with all our Navy stories!

"Get the hell off this ship!"

Pete Doe was a weatherman on the *Alpine*. He was from New England and we stayed in touch through our college days and on into our working and family years. He was also in the field of education so we had much in common. His wife died young, and when a son moved to North Carolina, Pete decided to move south to Kinston, North Carolina. George, Pete and I had great times together, fishing, eating and reminiscing about our past days. We told stories which were usually true, but sometimes embellished a bit! Pete's favorite tale was about an evening in San Diego. We celebrated a little too much and caused some confusion, but everything was worked out and ended well. Pete recalled and told in great detail about a typhoon we encountered. He told how we were given instructions about securing everything on the ship. The crew was directed to check every plank on the deck. Any loose board could rip off in a bad storm and result in a real disaster. It had been a scary time!

Another special friend was signalman John Lamb from Columbus, Ohio. He came on board the *Alpine* toward the end of the war as a late draftee. He was married and had two young children. We called him "the old man" because he was already more than thirty years old! John was a great guy, always happy and extremely friendly. He was a part of many interesting conversations aboard ship. After the war, we got together several times. His wife Gladys was also a pleasure to be with, and a great hostess! John had retired when we visited his home in Ohio and we began to tell our wives about some of our times together in the Navy.

Left to right: Jim Beasley, Pete Doe and Harry Weiss at the Beasley home on Emerald Isle, North Carolina, 2001.

28. Navy Friends

John started by telling me about comments made by his friends when he was planning his retirement. Everyone thought he should be making plans to do some traveling. He explained he did not want to waste his time traveling. They were puzzled and made many suggestions of places to go but he insisted he was not interested. Finally, John tried to defend himself by asking them, "Have you ever been to Guam? To Eniwetok? To Tsingtao? To Weihaiwei? I have been to all those places and a lot more. Why would I want to travel?" He said he never had to explain his choice again.

John told one story I had never heard but I could see it clearly in my mind. He began, "Early one morning I had duty and was standing on the deck looking out at the waves on the ocean as the sun began to rise. The captain came and stood a short distance from me. I looked over at him and commented, 'Isn't this a beautiful morning?' He quickly whirled around and in his sternest voice shouted, 'Who gave you permission to speak to me?' I was so scared all I could think was 'Jump overboard!' I gained my composure and saluted as I said, 'Yes, sir!' I learned a lesson to remember!"

Gladys and John Lamb at home in Columbus, Ohio, 1970.

Norman Vote was another special friend from the *Alpine*. We seemed to have a lot in common and became good friends immediately after he joined the crew. We went on leave many times together and had much to talk about when on the ship. As our lives moved on and the years passed we would call each other just to say, "Hello, how are things going?" He was from Michigan and returned there after he left the service. Elsie and I visited him and his delightful wife, Dottie, on several occasions and had a wonderful time. They lived near Lake Huron and he had a boat for fishing! On one trip when Norman and I returned from a day of fishing, I told Elsie we should move up there so I could catch salmon from the lake every day! He smoked enough fish each year to last him through the winter. We had driven our camper up there so he gave us smoked salmon to take home, but it never got to North Carolina—we ate the last bit going through Virginia! We lived too far from each other! They invited us to come sometime in the winter to see the Northern Lights, but we never did make it.

As time passed, I met with a good buddy, Jim Murphy, from Tacoma, Washington. We, along with our wives, met for lunch in Portland, Oregon, and discussed the past and made plans to meet again. Unfortunately, that did not come about.

Norman and Dottie Vote with Jim (right) at their home in Millersburg, Michigan, 1988.

28. Navy Friends

Hilda and Wally Andrews with Elsie (right) at the Beasley home in Banner Elk, North Carolina, 1992.

There was another Murphy, Bob, from Iowa with whom I kept in touch. We exchanged Christmas cards each year. On my way west I contacted him and had a good visit as we talked about the Navy and our present occupations—both of us had become teachers and administrators in public education.

Several years after leaving the Navy I failed to get my yearly card at Christmas from buddy Bill Henslee. I wondered about him but before I inquired of his whereabouts I got a letter from his mother telling me he had been killed in a car accident. He made it through the war but had some bad luck after he came home. I visited his grave site in Texas—sad.

Wally Andrews and I shared many good and bad times. We completed signal school together and both were assigned to the *Liscome Bay*. In addition to working and bunking together we went on liberty together. While in the hospital after our escapade of going to the admiral's office, we were to go for a physical check-up concerning our leave for rehabilitation. We made an oral contract—we would stay together no matter what! On the way to the doctor's office we picked up two tongue depressors. We thought if we were "hammered" on the back, we might start coughing and would spit up blood again.

If that happened we would probably not be discharged at the same time. I was called in first. When the doctor got out his hammer I put the tongue depressor under my tongue and bit down hard. He hit my back and it hurt terribly but I did not cough. He hit harder the second time and tears came to my eyes but I did not cough! He said, "Fine! You can be assigned to active duty after your thirty-day leave." I came out smiling and Andrews went in while I waited for him. From the waiting room I could hear Andrews coughing. He came out explaining, "Sam, it hurt so much I just couldn't help coughing." Andrews had to stay in the hospital for several more days before he was discharged. After his leave he was assigned to the hospital ship *Hope*. I did not see him again until after the war but did have the chance to speak to him by signals. Many years later, he and his wife Hilda came to North Carolina to spend a week with me and Elsie. I detected immediately he had not fared as well as I had in coping with our experiences in the Navy. We did not discuss the doctor's visit or other trying times we shared. I kept most of our conversation on our present activities.

There are many other stories I could tell. We had been on the *Liscome Bay* only a short time before our tragedy and our acquaintances were very limited. I had communicated with several of the survivors and had met with some of them but we never had the opportunity to really talk about the incident and tell our stories.

29

We Meet Again

In 1990 a special buddy from my Navy days phoned me. This friend from Lorain, Ohio, was Dale Wilker, who had been on the *Liscome Bay* and also on the *Alpine* with me. We kept in touch for more than forty years by mail, phone and personal visits. He and his wife visited with Elsie and me and we had been to their home for a most delightful visit. He was the fellow with whom I studied the map of the Pacific Islands while heading into battle aboard the *Alpine*. I knew immediately by his voice something big was going on. Excitedly he began to explain his reason for calling. He said a group of survivors from the *Liscome Bay* were organizing a reunion in October in Charleston, South Carolina, on the big aircraft carrier *Yorktown*. Had I heard about it and would I like to attend? I responded, "No, I had not heard about it, but do I want to go? Yes, definitely!"

I made the necessary contacts and in a few months I was a part of one of the most memorable occasions of my life. I was a spectator to a formal celebration aboard the *Yorktown*! Several of the survivors of the *Liscome Bay* held a service in honor of those who had died when our ship was torpedoed and sank. A Navy band was present to play the Navy anthem "Anchors Aweigh" and the Navy hymn "Eternal Father, Strong to Save." Albert Stoner was the acting president of the group and master of ceremonies. At the conclusion, wreaths were tossed into the water in remembrance of those who gave their all. After the band ended the ceremony and "Taps" was played, there was not a dry eye—not only among the survivors but among strangers who were just visiting as tourists.

Though only a few of the crew were in attendance at this first meeting, the celebration was a spark that caught fire and lasted for thirteen years. Several families of the casualties, headed by Lieutenant Finley Hall's family, had made plaques to present to the *Yorktown* for their museum which was focused on the carriers in World War II. The name of each one of the 642 men who lost his life in action while serving aboard the *Liscome Bay* was engraved on

"Get the hell off this ship!"

large bronze plaques. Both seamen and officers were honored for their heroic deeds.

At Charleston, Leonard Bohn, the acting secretary and treasurer of the group, volunteered to arrange for our first official meeting in the spring of 1991 in his hometown of Salina, Kansas. The USS *Liscome Bay* Association was well underway! Though many years had passed since the large number of good men had lost their lives in the tragedy, thoughts and visions remained in the minds of the fellow sailors as well as the families of those who were no longer among us. The gathering, in Charleston, was a solemn time to reunite the living and the dead and offered an opportunity to make certain those who were not with us in person would be remembered.

The meeting in Charleston was unusual. Since we had been on the ship for only three months before its sinking we were mostly strangers. However, we had so much in common we communicated easily. We talked and laughed (and sometimes cried) as we compared our experiences and became old friends. What a wonderful time we had! We all agreed this was what we had needed to open our minds and hearts to reality, to admit to ourselves and

On the *Yorktown* in Charleston, South Carolina, for the first gathering of the USS *Liscome Bay* Association in 1990. Nine survivors from eight states attended along with wives and other relatives. Men in back row, left to right: Leonard Bohm (KS), James Beasley (NC), Tony Kehl (WY), Albert Stoner (IN), James Honold (AR), Teofilo Trevino (TX), Joseph Lennon (FL) and Kenneth Harris (OR). Phelan Allee (TX) is kneeling in front.

29. We Meet Again

others what we had endured was not to be hidden and suppressed but to be openly talked about.

Our wives were amazing and amazed! They had never seen us act this way. Most had never heard any of what they were now learning about us. As one wife said, "You all act like a bunch of teenagers!" That is what we were when we last met. It made the sadness so much easier to absorb when shared with others who understood the feelings. This was the best thing that could have happened to me! I left the Navy in 1946 and now in 1990 I was starting where I left off. What a strange feeling!

I, as well as others, excitedly joined the group to make plans for the next year's gathering. We all took it upon ourselves to get in touch with as many survivors as possible to have a good turnout in Salina.

Each year we decided where we would hold the next reunion, while keeping in mind it might be difficult for some to travel a long distance. We elected officers every year, sometimes electing new members, but we held on to Leonard as secretary and treasurer. He did an outstanding job and kept in touch with everybody—no one could take his place!

We gained some members each year but unfortunately we lost some every year. Leonard knew if there was a death or illness and planned a special recognition for those who had passed or were not well at each gathering.

For the next twelve years, we held a reunion for the men who survived and for family members who were anxious to hear any information about their loved ones. Each event has its special memories for me.

October 1990 was the memorial service and organizational meeting, held aboard the carrier *Yorktown*. There were nine survivors in attendance, representing eight states. I will forever be thankful for the message from Dale who was unable to attend. I had not known any of those present while on the ship but that was unimportant as we had experienced the same horrible event.

Salina, Kansas, was the site for our meeting in April 1991. The same officers presided over the gathering: president, Albert Stoner; vice president, Don Walz; and secretary and treasurer Leonard Bohm. They were organized and well prepared to have a great reunion for the thrilled veterans who were able to attend. Salina was chosen mainly due to its central location and also because it would be easier for Leonard to make the arrangements. He joked about sailors meeting on dry ground, far from a large body of water! There were nineteen survivors from thirteen states. The true tales each one could tell were amazing. Al Stoner said he was five decks down when he was knocked off his feet and looked up through the open space to see the sky!

"Get the hell off this ship!"

Not only did the group have a chance to meet with someone who had suffered through the same terrible ordeal, we all enjoyed many sights and interesting trips that had been planned for the group's entertainment. It was difficult to say goodbye after three days together but there would be next year!

In May 1992 in Astoria, Oregon we had the largest reunion of all! There were thirty-five survivors. A lot of the crew had settled in that area after the war and it was also the port from which we had first sailed, so we had an exceptionally good turnout.

Tales of how each got off the ship circulated throughout the group. Many did not know their means of escape as they were unconscious at the time. Others told how some shipmate helped them off when they were unable to help themselves due to broken bones or other serious injuries. One said he was blown off the deck. This inspired a Spanish-speaking man from south Texas to tell his story in broken English. Teofilo Trevino said he was blown off with the first explosion. As he was floating in the water he looked up at the ship and said to himself, "I better get back up there; I'm a stretcher barrier and it looks like somebody will need my help!" Teo said he looked around

The USS *Liscome Bay* Association, Astoria, Oregon, in 1992. Back row, left to right: Tony Kehl, Irvin Jones, Willard Pinder, Tim Woodham, Leonard Bohm, Lester Bush, Teofilo Trevino, Albert Adam. Front row, left to right: Phelan Allee, James Beasley, Paul von Kempf, Roger Freeman, Charles Breeden, Donald Walz, K. J. Harris, Charles Benson. Several members were not present for the photograph.

29. We Meet Again

for a rope and quickly scrambled back aboard the ship. Just as he stood up, there was another explosion and down into the water he went for the second time. This time when he looked up he said, "If anybody needs a stretcher, he'll have to get it himself!"

Many family members of those who died when the ship was sunk attended this reunion. They all praised the group who had done this great service for the survivors and told how much they appreciated being invited to attend and to meet their loved one's shipmates. As K. J. Harris, a survivor from Oregon, expressed it, "The best part of the reunion was the history of how it all took place and the healing it brought to those in attendance."

There was a sad note to the reunion—Al Stoner, the former president, died just two weeks before the gathering in Astoria. His wife attended and thanked everyone for their help in continuing his dream. She said, "Al would be so pleased and I'm sure he is looking down on us now."

Many interesting activities were planned for the three days in Astoria and everyone enjoyed seeing that the old Port of Astoria building was still standing. It had been a long time since August 1943 and the commissioning of the *Liscome Bay*! We all hoped we would meet again next year.

In May 1993 we met in Hannibal, Missouri. Seventeen *Liscome Bay* survivors came together for a fifty-year reunion. We had many from the Midwest and the East to attend for the first time and we were happy to have them join us. However, there were many from the West who were unable to make the trip. They were greatly missed. Every reunion became more precious as we felt closer to those friends we never knew until recently.

The stories continued to be shared. Many of them were of heroic deeds. One seaman told how an officer saved his life by holding his head above water when he was unable to help himself. Many gave credit to shipmates they did not know but who helped them survive. Others made funny remarks. One survivor, looking at the photo of the *Liscome Bay* exploding, said, "I don't know how I got off. Hey, that looks like me flying through the air as a bright light!" We laughed.

The activities planned for our entertainment included a boat ride on the Mississippi riverboat *Mark Twain*. We all felt like little boys riding on an open train as we toured some of Tom Sawyer territory with a guide to tell us about the town of Hannibal. There was always a great banquet the last night of the meeting and this was no exception. Mark Twain was our guest speaker! Again we left our friends with the pledge to attend again next year!

Fredericksburg, Texas, was the destination for another *Liscome Bay*

"Get the hell off this ship!"

reunion in May 1994. This meeting was being held at the Admiral Nimitz Museum for a specific purpose. The USS *Liscome Bay* Survivors Association had a memorial to present to the museum there. We planned a service with K.J. Harris as master of ceremonies and with the color guard of Austin, Texas, helping. I was the designated representative of the organization to make the presentation. The plaque had a picture of the *Liscome Bay* and appropriate words to be placed on the wall in the path where other similar plaques had been placed. I read the presentation which included, "We are gathered here to remember and honor the aircraft carrier *Liscome Bay* and the men who served her." Al Stoner's wife unveiled the plaque. After the benediction by our own chaplain Jack Krantz, a bugler from the band played "Taps," bringing tears to many eyes. A number of relatives of the lost were also present for the dedication. I overheard a survivor speaking to a brother of a non-survivor about the torpedo strike. "Our faces revealed we were scared to death, then someone yelled, 'Get busy! Don't give up!' We jumped into action. Your brother was one of the many unlucky ones that day."

The planning committee had a busy schedule of activities including a trip to President Johnson's ranch. There were thirteen survivors in attendance, some new and some old members. Each year Leonard informed us of the deaths during the past year of our comrades and also told of members who could not be with us due to ill health. Again, we sadly bid farewell—not good-bye!

In May 1995 we gathered at Corpus Christi, Texas. The aircraft carrier *Lexington*, after being retired from active duty, was anchored there. What a time we all had pretending we were young and active and in the Navy once more! A big banner on the side of the ship greeted us: "WELCOME ABOARD USS *LEXINGTON*." Though only twelve survivors were in attendance we had a very good gathering and told more tales!

One story a fellow seaman told was similar to an experience of mine. He said when he arrived home he was talking with a neighbor about the sinking of his ship and the neighbor said, "We had a terrible time during those fighting days. We couldn't get gas, sugar was rationed and there were no silk hose!" He said, "I said no more. I could not compete with the hard times and problems she had endured!"

Des Moines, Iowa, was our location for a fall reunion in September 1996. There had been a conflict for the annual spring meeting and the fall timing was great for Iowa. There were twelve present to enjoy the fellowship and the usual good entertainment by the planning committee. The botanical gardens were outstanding!

29. We Meet Again

It is impossible to tell all the great things we did at each meeting. There was usually a shopping trip planned for the ladies and a museum trip for everyone. I mentioned the banquet that was held on the last evening—it was always the highlight of the gathering. Besides a great meal and a guest speaker, there was an auction to close out the evening. Everyone brought some item or items to sell to raise money for the ship's store. Many were homemade by the survivors or their wives. I don't know who enjoyed the auction more, the bidders or the auctioneer, K.J. Harris!

April 1997 came upon me quickly but I knew I would not miss going to Independence, Missouri, for another great reunion! Anything else on the schedule would have to wait. I was very much an admirer of President Harry Truman. I think his bold decision to drop the atomic bomb on Japan saved my life! There were twelve survivors who attended. Some new members were welcomed and some regular attendees were present but several regulars were unable to attend.

Though we visited a number of beautiful estates and fine mansions I was most impressed with the simple home of President Truman. It was a house like any of us might own. We even walked the streets he walked when he was taking his daily morning stroll. A local impersonator gave the evening speech at the banquet. He was dressed like Mr. Truman, cane, glasses, suit and all. He was about his size and build and even his voice sounded like Truman's. We were amazed and very impressed with the resemblance!

We were honored to have Lieutenant Hall's daughter with us. Mary Jane Wiesler and hus-

Mary Jane Hall Wiesler and husband Jim, 1997.

"Get the hell off this ship!"

band Jim were great supporters of the *Liscome Bay*'s organization and attended the reunions when possible. There were other family members of the men who were lost in the terrible tragedy. Their attendance always made our celebrations more important to everyone.

In April 1998 we returned to Charleston, South Carolina, and received a grand tour of the carrier *Yorktown*. It is docked at Patriots Point and is open to the public as a museum. We were honored and treated like royalty by all those who were in charge of our visit. The *Yorktown* was the carrier that welcomed four of the Wildcats from our lost patrol crew the evening before the *Liscome Bay* was torpedoed. (They directed the fifth plane to the nearby *Lexington* and it also made a safe landing.)

I especially enjoyed touring the big carrier. It was so much like my former home, but on a much larger scale. I checked out the signalman's area—the flags and the lights—and wondered, "Could I send messages again or have I forgotten how? I would be much slower but I think I could manage."

Charleston is a beautiful city for sightseeing. We chartered a bus and toured all over the area. The historic churches, the beautiful homes, the view from the Battery, and of course Fort Sumter gave us a feeling of the old South.

I arranged to find time to talk with Bill Fisher, one of the few I remembered from the early days of the *Liscome Bay*. We not only talked about what happened

Jim Beasley (left) and Bill Fisher at the USS *Liscome Bay* reunion at Patriot's Point, South Carolina, 1998, with the aircraft carrier *Yorktown* in the background.

134

29. We Meet Again

Paul von Kempf demonstrates signals for landing a plane on a small carrier, 1998.

to our ship but we went back to the glory days of the "Listing Lizzy." We shared good memories of long ago. I also spent time with Gerald Goss. We were aboard the *Alpine* together. Soon after leaving the Navy I visited him at his family's home in Pennsylvania. He was a great guy and a good friend. We corresponded for some time but then lost touch. We had much to tell each other of events throughout the past fifty years. A new acquaintance, Paul von Kempt, and I had a great time together. He was a signalman with the flight crew and demonstrated his signals for landing a plane with flags on the small runway. He had a difficult task, to say the least! The pilot and the signalman had to fully understand each other's signs. It took nerves of steel for a pilot to take off or land on our short runway. The heavy torpedo bombers would drop completely out of sight at the end of the deck in a takeoff. We would finally see it coming into view flying just above the water. We would give a loud cheer! Paul said it was nerve-wracking.

I heard a number of inspiring, heroic and courageous stories with which I could identify. Others were terribly gruesome, frightening and sad, like these: "I watched helplessly as a fellow sailor struggled near the ship, he disappeared under the water" and "I stood on the deck ready to dive into the ocean when

"Get the hell off this ship!"

I saw a shipmate jump into the blazing fire on top of the water. I saw him instantly burn to death. I had no choice, and with great uncertainty, I jumped quickly and stayed under the water and swam like the devil." Everyone smiled when we heard humorous stories like this one: "I was swimming around in the Pacific Ocean with a bunch of turkeys—our Thanksgiving Dinner. I was not very hungry."

The flight deck of the *Yorktown* was a good place to have our banquet. All arrangements were made to set up tables among the many memorials and we were served a delightful meal for our final evening together. Good Southern food and hospitality made our visitors from the West and the North feel at home. The auction was successful and our treasury was replenished. We were confident that Leonard would begin working on next year's reunion as soon as he finalized this one by sending reports to all members whether they were in attendance or not. We made our farewells vowing to meet again next year!

San Diego was our chosen destination for April 1999. We had spent more time there than probably any other port and we were happy to return. A

The USS *Liscome Bay* reunion in San Diego, 1999, with 24 survivors in attendance.

29. We Meet Again

The 1999 *Liscome Bay* reunion in San Diego. Left to right: Robert Price, Jim Beasley and Dale Wilker.

Jim Beasley (left) and Tim Woodham pointing to the name of the *Liscome Bay* on a plaque near the dock in San Diego, 1999.

number of our members of the *Liscome Bay* Association had retired there so the turnout was very good. Twenty-five survivors attended, some for the first time. The weather was perfect and San Diego is a gem for tourists! Our home base was the Best Western. From there we toured the city by bus, trolley, and boat, visiting more places than I can list here. Being sailors, we especially liked the waterfront and the cruise. We ate at a great restaurant, Anthony's, and saw the historic ship *Star of India*. Of course we had to see the famous San Diego Zoo, Point Loma, and Coronado.

Every day was busy with interesting activities and most of us—the "old seamen"—were ready to get back to the motel and visit with our buddies in the hospitality room. At every reunion we kept a room available during reasonable hours to relax and talk, to snack and have something to drink, and make plans for future gatherings. We needed more rest now than we needed when we were young and foolish!

New stories of heroism, sacrifice and horror were told. A member of the group had a copy of an article by a journalist who quoted a sailor from a nearby ship as describing what he saw as a "fiery holocaust" that he never wanted to see again!

Left to right: Tim Woodham, Leonard Bohm and Phelan Allee at the *Liscome Bay* reunion at Pensacola, Florida, 2000.

29. We Meet Again

In May 2000, Pensacola, Florida, was the location for our annual reunion. During the tour of the city, the Museum of Naval Aviation was probably the most impressive to us. Seeing all the planes, Wildcat fighters and Avenger bombers with their wings folded back, took my breath away. I looked over at Tim Woodham and it was obvious he was feeling sentimental also. He had worked specifically with the aircraft that were on the *Liscome Bay*. I recalled how shocked I had been in 1943 when all those planes were brought on deck, wings folded back, placed on the large elevators and sent down to lower decks! Many military men vowed the air power supplied by the carriers won the war. By 2000 the planes as well as the ships had been greatly improved and we could not comprehend everything we saw on the new planes.

Twelve survivors, many of their wives and several grown children enjoyed sunny Pensacola. The time seemed too short! The banquet was very nice and as usual the auction was a lot of fun. We said our farewells until next year.

April 2001 found us gathering in the entertainment resort Branson, Missouri. Thirteen survivors attended and we probably had the most family

The USS *Liscome Bay* reunion at Branson, Missouri, 2001. Thirteen survivors and many family members after a ride on the showboat *The Branson Belle*.

"Get the hell off this ship!"

members there of any reunion! Was it because of the stage shows we would see or did our children think we needed supervision?

We toured the town and surrounding area by bus and train and we had an outstanding cruise aboard a large showboat, *The Branson Belle*, on Table Rock Lake. It had been hard to decide which shows to attend but the committee made good choices. We learned we had a stage star in our midst. Phelan Allee volunteered to go up and help the performers entertain. And entertain, he did! He stole the show with his singing and jokes. We loved it and so did he! The banquet was held at the Ramada Inn downtown. Everyone had a great time being together again and plans and promises were made for another year.

April 2002 was a return to Hannibal, Missouri. We were happy to go there again and many new members requested the location. Tom Sawyer's hometown had a fascination for the boy in us! Hannibal is small and easy to get around. It is centrally located and near water for the old sailors. We had great tours and heard many stories about Tom Sawyer and his life on the Mississippi River. The cruise on the river was aboard the *Mark Twain*. We were treated to a concert on the calliope, with real steam whistles played with keys!

The fourteen members, wives, kinfolk and friends had a great time! The photos show many smiles and lots of laughter. The banquet and the auction were delightful. We were now well acquainted with our newfound old friends and could display a sense of humor without offending someone.

Elsie and Jim Beasley, 2001.

29. We Meet Again

There was one sad note we discussed at our business and planning meeting. The truth was that we were a dying organization. Did we want to just fade away or go out in glory? We were all growing older and were losing many survivors every year. It was becoming more difficult to plan a meeting and to travel. What should we do? We decided to get all of our collections of memorabilia, notes, papers and photos together and donate everything to a naval museum. We were aware that the ship *Midway* would be docked at San Diego and turned into a museum. We contacted those in charge and they assured us that space would be available for our donation. They would process and display it in a way to honor the *Liscome Bay* and its men. The decision was made to follow through with that idea of donating everything we had collected to the *Midway*. We left Hannibal with a feeling of sadness but with pride in our accomplishments over the last thirteen years. We waved and called, "So long until we meet again next year in San Diego!"

April 2003 we gathered in beautiful San Diego. Elsie and I took our camper and camped in a nice campground east of San Diego several days before the meeting. We wanted to be early so we would not miss anything! When others arrived we moved into town and stayed with the group at the Seven Seas Best Western Lodge, our headquarters. The hospitality room was set up immediately and was constantly in use. Since this would be our last time to meet many chose to stay and visit with each other rather than participate in planned activities. However, the tour of the city was interesting. We visited La Jolla and the pretty and busy beach, went up on Soledad Mountain where the Mt. Soledad Veterans Memorial Cross is located, saw the Carousel at Seaport Village, and made a trip to Tijuana, Mexico. The survivors commented on Tijuana and how it had changed since they had visited there about sixty years ago.

The officers of the USS *Liscome Bay* Association turned over all materials we had about the *Liscome Bay* and the minutes and collections of our organization to the curator of the *Midway*. At the final gathering we were assured everything would be displayed in the museum in honor of the *Liscome Bay* and its crew when the *Midway* was docked. We took pride in working with our fellow survivors and knew it had been a blessing to all who had been a part of the association.

As the sixteen survivors departed they were sad not to be anticipating another reunion next year but rejoiced to have been able to reunite for thirteen wonderful gatherings! "Who knows? We may meet again!" was the comment made by one of the officers. All agreed.

"Get the hell off this ship!"

The USS *Liscome Bay* Survivors Association final reunion held in San Diego in 2003. Standing, left to right: George McFedries, Joe Blankenship, Willard Pinder, Leonard Bohm, Edward Schmitt, Bill Fisher, John Beymer, Tim Woodham, Willard Youtz and Donald Cruse. Seated, left to right: K. J. Harris, Roger Freeman, Edward Jonas, Phelan Allee, Paul von Kempf, Sam Beaumont and Jim Beasley. Not pictured: Edward Ferguson.

Leonard Bohm, our dedicated secretary and treasurer, and one of the original organizers of the association, was present for every one of the reunions. Phelan Allee and I were the only other survivors who attended all the gatherings. Many others missed only one or two of the meetings. Our life aboard the *Liscome Bay* only lasted from August 7, 1943, to November 24, 1943, but made an impression that will last a lifetime! We are buddies forever.

30

Remembering

When I arrived home in 1946 with a vow to put the past four years behind me, I did not realize how difficult that would be. There were daytime thoughts to conquer but the nightmares were beyond my control and were usually extremely disturbing. Any sudden or loud noise, crying or shouting threw me into some automatic response I often later regretted. My sister was proud of the bright kimono I had given her and she deliberately paraded around the house to show it off. Seeing it on her had a strange effect on me and I left the room. I never saw her wear it again. Other gifts I had brought home for family members disappeared from view. I knew I had a problem to deal with.

In June I gathered my belongings and left for college. I was eager to get on with my plans to further my education. It took several months going to classes to get into a study mode but school and my part-time jobs kept me occupied physically and mentally. Few fellow veterans discussed their military experiences but their level of maturity was obvious to professors and younger students. The whole atmosphere on campus changed with the return of the veterans as we were constantly reminded! Frequently I thought of how lucky I was to be a survivor and have the opportunity of attending college.

November was always a difficult month for me. I did not attempt to explain why I became so unpredictable and at times irrational. My wife thought I was concerned about another birthday coming up and getting older! She tried to have a special celebration for me. The children were taught to be thoughtful and to tread lightly. She was also puzzled about the time I spent in my office area alone. I was not unhappy with the family or my circumstances—quite the contrary. I just needed time for thought and contemplation. There were so many ideas in my mind and it took solitude to deal with each one. I wondered, "Why did I survive? What am I supposed to do?" Sometimes I praised myself for helping to prevent Japan from reaching its goal to conquer the world.

There were memories I enjoyed recalling. I thought many times of the islanders who fought desperately to hold on to their paradise and their effort

"Get the hell off this ship!"

to show us their appreciation for our help. Tiger eyes were plentiful on one small island we visited and we traded our mattress covers for the gems. We were happy with the trade and so were the natives.

On one occasion when we had completed our battle assignment and were in dock for supplies and a little rest, we were granted a leave from the ship for a beach party. Some of the islanders came over to watch us unload the cases of beer and boxes of snacks. They seemed fascinated as we yelled at one another while playing ball, swimming, or lying on the beach. When a sailor started the music, a crowd began to gather at a distance. Our music was totally different from any they knew and it was turned up very loud! The man in charge of the music must have been from the South. He played "Guitar Boogie" and "Dueling Banjos" by Arthur Smith over and over again. Finally, some Yankee yelled a threat to him if he didn't turn "that stuff" off!

Sometimes I thought of the stewards on the ship. They were African Americans who helped in the officers' quarters and did the kitchen duty. All blacks were segregated from the whites in World War II and performed jobs considered to be servants' duties. But let me tell you, they were good fighters and loyal to the United States.

On both ships I got acquainted with some of the stewards. In the signal shack we drank lots and lots of coffee—more than we were allotted. Day and night we had hot, black coffee boiling to assure us we were on our toes and alert for some signal coming our way. When our supply got low someone asked a steward friend for help. Many times when I went for coffee, a cook offered me a steak left over from the officers' dinner. They were helpful to us and good sailors!

There was one steward on the *Liscome Bay* who had survived the surprise attack on Pearl Harbor. With no regard for his own safety, Dorie Miller manned a gun and was decorated for his heroic actions. He received the Navy Cross and had a ship named for him. He was not so lucky on the *Liscome Bay*; he lost his life when it was torpedoed.

In my quiet time I wrote letters to my friends from all over the United States. I sent Christmas greetings to Captain Reilly and his wife in Seattle, Washington. She responded with a very nice personal note telling me about her family and inquiring about mine. We exchanged these greetings for several years. She told me of the captain's death from a heart attack in 1958. Upon retirement he had been given the rank of rear admiral. I felt very special when I received the letter but also very sad.

I constantly searched for information concerning the sinking of the *Lis-*

30. Remembering

come Bay. During the war little was written about it, but more and more attention was given to the incident as the years went by. I collected newspaper articles, books that mentioned the ship, magazine stories, and official naval records and photos. I read and reread the accounts.

Historian Samuel Eliot Morison wrote thirteen volumes about the naval operations in World War II (seven were devoted to the action in the Pacific). He dedicated volume seven "To the Memory of Henry Maston Mullinix." It covered the action from June 1942 to April 1944. Speaking of Admiral Mullinix, Morrison states, "He was one of the most gifted, widely experienced and beloved of the Navy's admirals."

After reading about so many of our great leaders like Nimitz and MacArthur, naming only two, I know they deserve all the credit that has been given them for their judgment and knowledge in those difficult and uncertain times. I praise all who were in battle, however I do not think enough credit has been given to those who for days, weeks and even months kept the troops with fuel, equipment and ammunition, not to mention food, clothing and medicine. Remarkable!

Some of the most interesting accounts concerning the short travels of the *Liscome Bay* came from the ship's newspaper which was published during the time we were on board. Volume I, issue I, dated Saturday September 4, 1943, stated everything was going smoothly after the first four weeks. Captain Wiltsie said, "Keep up the good works!" The paper had not been named so $5 was offered to the person with the best idea for its name. Chaplain Carley was the editor and his office was in the library. He encouraged everyone to submit something for the paper. It carried informative notices, jokes, news articles, schedules for badminton and volleyball, and also the names and times of the movies to be shown. The cartoon drawings were typical and Navy-inspired. Upon seeing the paper for the first time, I thought, "Is this the way the navy operates?" Each issue had a "written portrait" of one of the officers, and Chaplain Carley wrote an editorial each week. After some rough seas and the sickness that goes along with it, his editorial was titled "Let Us Learn to Love the Sea!" Another editorial I enjoyed was "Character of a Happy Ship." I thought we fit that description real well.

Chaplain Carley was a busy man! He was sincerely interested in every man on the ship. He held weekly worship services for each religious group and stressed the importance of faith regardless of one's religion. A joint service was conducted before any major battle or potentially dangerous encounter. He used the newspaper as a means of constant inspiration by writing some

"Get the hell off this ship!"

words of wisdom. When he interviewed Admiral Mullinix for an article, he quoted him as saying, "This ship will make history."

The name selected for the ship's paper from the many entries was *LisBay Totem Pole* in honor of the Indians who lived on the Liscome Bay in Alaska. I have several issues including the last copy printed, Volume I, issue 10, November 18, 1943. In one issue we were given a list of Japanese words to learn in preparation for our arrival in Japan. "Sayonara," good-bye in English, was the only word I wanted to learn.

I was interested in knowing what happened to the Japanese submarine # I-175 that sent the torpedo our way, making a direct hit. I researched several sources and learned Lieutenant Commodore Tabata was the officer in charge. He took his sub deep down below the surface of the water to avoid the depth charges our ships were sending to destroy his vessel. We were deploying the charges quickly and constantly but did not hit him at that time. Some of our ships sank the sub later but before it did damage to another United States ship. The depth charges were frequent and loud in the water and many men floating around the area had damaged ear drums, including me. I found con-

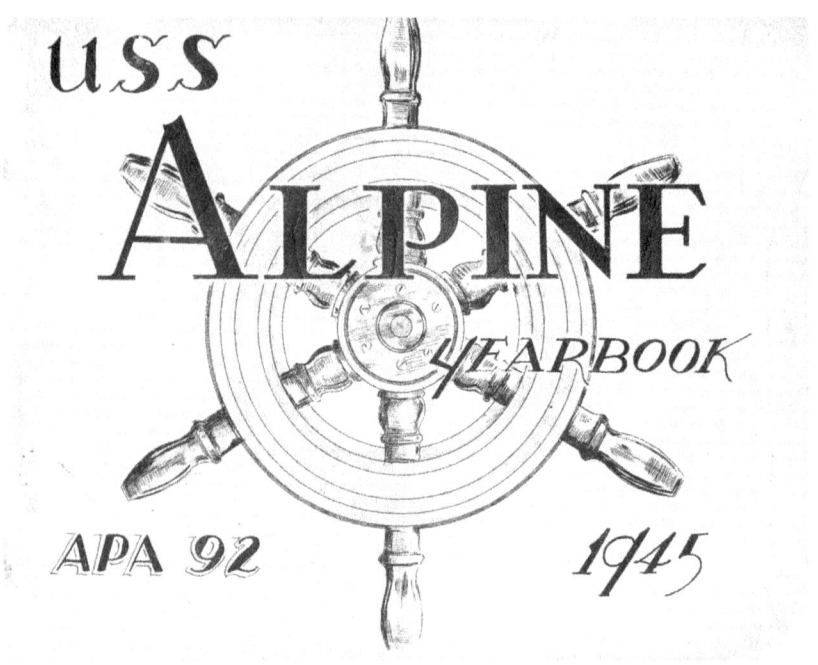

The *Alpine* yearbook cover.

30. Remembering

flicting stories of the time and place of the sinking of the sub but the Japanese verified its disappearance.

A yearbook for the crew was printed in 1945 aboard the *Alpine*. It contained the roster with a short biographical sketch of each officer. There was a history of the ship and information from the ship's logs. Over and over again I looked at the photos and the names of the crew members. Activities on and off the ship were shown either in photographs or drawings by very dedicated and talented staff members. I have spent many hours enjoying every page of the book.

In my solitude I found pleasure in writing my recollections of the many good and bad times I had experienced. That helped to inspire me to put this book together. I am told it probably aided me in accepting and dealing with my mental and emotional stability during these sixty-plus years.

I now have quite a collection of published articles and books as well as personal accounts from both observers and many participants in the war in the Pacific in World War II. The most important paper I have is the one issued by the War Department naming the survivors from the sinking of the *Liscome Bay*. James C. Beasley is on the list!

I learned from the official records in Washington, D.C., that my first home in the Navy, the USS *Liscome Bay*, was remembered with great honor and distinction. It was the first "baby flat top" to be lost as a result of enemy action in the Pacific. She was the only ship lost in the Gilbert Islands operation. The extensive damage she received caused her to sink in twenty-three minutes. The gallant crew received high praise for the courage and effort amid much confusion and destruction. On board were 911 men and 53 officers. Among the 591 missing were the ship's commander, Captain I. D. Wiltsie, and Rear Admiral H. M. Mullinix. She earned only one battle star but she gave her all!

I kept the cards of authorization issued to me when I crossed the 180th meridian on the *Liscome Bay* and on the *Alpine*. I also kept my dog tags, keys, many photos and other reminders of my Navy days. My ribbons and rewards have been framed and hang above my desk. I do not think of them as personal rewards but as my contribution to a team that helped to win the war. I participated in six major battles and served twenty-one months outside of the United States. I was awarded the Purple Heart for my injuries suffered when my ship was sunk. I treasure all the honors I received but have a special feeling for the World War II Victory Medal! Those years represent an important time in my life.

31

The Grand Finale

I became the "normal" or "average" young man with a wife and children. I worked long hours as an educator while buying a home and trying to save for the coming years. I dreamed of sending the children to college and having enough for our own retirement. We were all healthy and eager to move forward. The years passed quickly!

Elsie and I continued to work in the public schools with plans to have enough of a nest egg to retire comfortably in North Carolina. We arranged to buy her parent's home in Banner Elk where we hoped to spend the summers. We later built a small cottage at Emerald Isle for the winter months. It proved to be a good arrangement for all the family. The children and grandchildren enjoyed the beach in the summer and usually came to the mountains for a snowy Christmas. We enjoyed our daughters and their families. There were four grandsons and three granddaughters—all within six years from the oldest to the youngest. We had many great times together!

In June of 1989 the children planned a big celebration for our 40th Wedding Anniversary. We followed that with a Golden Wedding Anniversary in 1999! Luckily we were still around and in good health in 2009 for a 60th Celebration. We were living in Newland, only ten miles from Banner Elk, and notified many friends about the big event. Among the guests were relatives from near and far as well as many friends we had made throughout the years.

We were pleasantly surprised when a buddy from the *Liscome Bay* and his wife showed up! Phelan and Dorothy Allee drove all the way from Houston, Texas to help us celebrate. They spent the night with us and we had a wonderful time telling tales, laughing and eating!

When I was at Emerald Isle I began to attend meetings with World War II veterans who met at Morehead City. Many soldiers, sailors, marines, airman and coast guardsmen had retired in the area and had formed a group who got together at least once every three months. They met at a local seafood

31. The Grand Finale

Elsie and Jim Beasley enjoying seven wonderful grandchildren. Left to right: James and Elizabeth Rutledge; Matthew, David and Rachel Burks; and Charlotte and Jonathon Bissette (May 1987).

restaurant for lunch, had their business meeting and a local speaker who told of his military experiences. Elsie went as my guest and we both enjoyed the war stories, the friendship and of course the great seafood!

The director of the Veterans Association in the area also attended the meetings. He helped anyone who had a question or some specific need from the VA. In talking with him I learned I was overdue for compensation for the injuries I had received in battle. (The ones I had refused to wait three days in the hospital to have verified by a doctor.) He encouraged me to come to his office and fill out the proper forms. With his help I was awarded a small

Jim and Elsie Beasley at their 60th wedding anniversary (June 2009).

"Get the hell off this ship!"

pension and was enrolled for medical care when needed. That became a blessing to me in my "old age."

I was accepted into this active group and welcomed with open arms. They invited me to go with them to Washington, D.C., to visit the World War II memorial. I had hoped to see it but never dreamed I could go with fellow veterans! The trip and visit had so much more meaning being in the company of those who really understood what it meant and represented.

The Honor Flight of Southeastern North Carolina, sponsored by area organizations and personal donations, made the trip on September 22, 2010. One hundred and eight veterans were chosen to fly from New Bern to Washington. I had the honor of being in the group! We left New Bern early in the morning by a chartered plane with many volunteers along with us to help if needed. Some of us were in wheelchairs or needed assistance walking, while others were very frail or needed help with medication. I was among the fortunate. I could walk at a brisk pace and did not need assistance of any kind while on the trip. We were "pampered" in every way! The trip was an "all expense paid" with no cost to any veteran.

Honor Flight to Washington, D.C., September 2010. Jim Beasley is pictured standing behind the man in the white shirt.

31. The Grand Finale

World War II Memorial in Washington, D.C., 2010.

It had been many years since I had visited our Capitol and other memorials located there. We all enjoyed the bus tour of the city to see the many historical sites there. However our main focus was on the World War II Memorial—the nation's way of honoring us! We were impressed and became rather emotional when viewing the special tribute to North Carolina. We were served a good lunch and had time to talk with our Senators and have photographs made.

On the way back to New Bern we were also treated to a good meal on the plane. Each of us received a packet of notes, letters and mementos to read on the way home. It was reassuring to know we were appreciated for our service many years ago. Upon arriving back in New Bern we were greeted by community supporters of all ages with gifts, hugs and encouraging words of thanks. I was pleased beyond words to have been invited on this Honor Flight. It was actually the first time I had been welcomed with a cheering crowd after returning from the war. After more than sixty years I was given an enthusiastic "Welcome Home"!

I experienced with pride the "Grand Finale" to my service in the United States Navy!

Epilogue
By Elsie Lowe Beasley

After the Honor Flight to Washington, D.C. October 2010, Jim participated in the annual Veterans Day Celebration parade in November at Morehead City, N.C. We planned to stay at our cottage in Emerald Isle for the remainder of the winter.

At the end of February we attended the Sunday morning worship service at the Salterpath Methodist Church, had lunch at home, and went for a walk on the beach. At Jim's suggestion we sat down on a bench overlooking the ocean. I knew he was tired and needed a brief rest. He commented on the beautiful day and the peaceful ocean as we watched the slight ripple of the waves as they met the sand on the beach. He began to talk or as he expressed it, "think out loud." He asked me if I thought the Preacher's message fit the day, as he recalled its title "Be Happy and Enjoy Life Each and Every Day." As we sat on the bench mostly in silence observing the vast blue ocean, Jim spoke of how he had been greatly blessed and questioned whether he deserved the many good things that had come his way.

In February there are few people on the beach so we were basically alone. A lone sea gull darted back and forth over head. Almost an hour had passed when Jim concluded his thoughts with this comment, "This must be the most beautiful place in the world and it is for me to enjoy!" After another slight pause, he said "Let's go back and watch the NASCAR races on TV." Early the next morning, February 28, 2011, Jim passed away at his beloved home on Emerald Isle, N.C.

Jim had worked on this book with dedication—and pleasure—off and on for a long time and I knew I could not drop the project. After he had put so much of himself into writing his treasured memories, how could I just let it die? Since I was his audience and sounding board all these years I was the only person to follow through with his efforts. With his many pages of manuscripts, his extensive notes and photographs, as well as the stacks of printed

Epilogue

material he collected of people and events, I am attempting to finish the book by organizing the information he wanted to publish, in his story-telling style. Everyone who knew Jim knew he loved to tell stories! Some of the ideas he intended to finish writing about I will relate to you here as accurately as I can.

In speaking on the phone with Norman Vote after Jim's death, he took me by surprise when he made the following comment, "Do you realize we were only eighteen years old when we went into the Navy? It was quite an experience for a young man!" Norman was not aware of Jim's intention to name his memoirs *I Was Only Eighteen*. Comradeship is spiritually deep!

Other expressions I heard Jim comment on were often repeated by a Navy friend, "I left the Navy but it never left me." "Were my Navy years a dream or a nightmare?" "Just think what I learned in the Navy."

Two special friends who survived the tragedy of the *Liscome Bay* were Pete Umbehagen and Wally Andrews. After the formation of the Liscome Bay Association and the annual meetings, Jim made a special effort to inform and encourage each to attend, but neither of them ever came.

Pete Umbehagen lived in Louisiana. He had gone there to work in the oil industry in the Gulf area. He had a devoted wife and several children. Jim knew from Pete's letters he had a number of difficult events happen to him and he was not in good health. Jim stated, "I must get him to attend one of our Reunions or visit him in Louisiana. We need to catch up with each other—he was a good Navy friend." One time we did visit his hometown and found where he lived, but the house was empty. A neighbor told us he moved near one of his children but did not know where. All efforts to track him were unsuccessful. Later, Jim received a letter from a daughter saying Pete had passed on and when she had found Jim's address, she wanted to tell him the sad news. It was a very nice letter which Jim answered immediately, expressing his sympathy and then he placed her letter with his valuable papers.

Wally Andrews was another signalman from the *Liscome Bay* that Jim tried to persuade to attend the Reunions but was not successful. He lived in Indiana. Wally had some lasting effects as a result of his Navy experiences and he relied on professional help to treat his depression. Among Jim's notes I found the following thoughts: "Wally and Hilda came to North Carolina one summer for a visit. We picnicked on the Grandfather Mountain and visited several other interesting places in the area. Then Elsie and I drove them to the NC coast to our cottage at Emerald Isle for a few days. A Navy vessel was docked there and was open to the public. With our Navy credentials we

Epilogue

were taken on a special tour. What a visit! Seeing all the new improvements and strange developments on the ship was amazing. The radar and other special equipment was recessed, all the guns were hidden and everything operated by pushing a button! We had a great time." After spending the whole afternoon on the ship, Hilda commented on staying there over night. Jim and Wally thought it a great idea! We were delighted to have them come to visit us. We continued to keep in touch.

Jim and I had met at Catawba College in Salisbury, N.C., three years after his discharge from the Navy. I knew he was one of those vets who had invaded our college and changed everything on campus! He seldom spoke of his days in the military—good or bad. After we married, I became agitated at times at his unexplained silence and seemingly disinterest in our family activities but as the years passed we adjusted to our differences. He tried to be more consistent in his actions and I learned to be patient and ignore unusual situations.

Only after the gatherings with fellow crewmen from his ship the *Liscome Bay*, did Jim begin to talk freely about his Navy experiences. I was shocked to hear of the things he had been involved in and wondered how he had suppressed it so long. As he told in great detail of the horrible events he had been a part of, I became a better listener with an understanding of his feelings. Frequently he read aloud comments from articles written in books, magazines or newspapers by someone who expressed ideas similar to his.

One special article he read and reread was by Al Silverman in a publication called *True Action* written in December 1943. He spoke of the sinking of the *Liscome Bay* as the "tragic story of WWII's greatest naval disaster—644 seamen all in the water all dead." Silverman continued, "You couldn't say much for her (the *Liscome Bay*). She wasn't beautiful—built like a tub; she couldn't take it—one torpedo finished her. But she and her crew wrote the book on what it is to die with courage" He tells of a seaman on board the battleship *New Mexico* who witnessed the tragic event and commented about the crew "Heroism was the rule, not the exception, among those who survived the initial blast on the *Liscome Bay*—Heroism and blind, dogged courage."

The reunions were important yearly events for me as well as for Jim. We wives enjoyed being together and discussing how important the annual gatherings were to our husbands. We began to understand the unpredictable behavior of our mates! Many great friendships were made or renewed each year.

Dorthy Bohm was Leonard's "right hand." Without her, he would have

Epilogue

been unable to do the great and outstanding job he did as the organization's secretary. Dorthy was always a pleasure to be around and worked with Leonard from day one to make things move smoothly.

Helen Woodham, Tim's wife, was a lovely person and enjoyed each and every reunion she attended. We greatly missed her when she was no longer with us.

Dorothy Allee, Chaplain Phelan's wife was a "doer"! She was always busy helping with preparations or finding a "first-time" attendee to make a new friend. When Phelan, the entertainer in the crowd, played a joke on someone (usually himself), she helped him. Like the time in San Diego when he told everyone he was going to Long Beach to look for a girl he met on the beach when in the Navy some forty years ago—she said "I'll go help you find her!" She became a friend for life.

Vera Freeman, wife of Roger, and I had many great conversations about our camping experiences. We both loved to travel in our campers. She and Roger were from the state of Washington so she told me of many great places to camp there and I shared my favorite places in the eastern part of the country. The four of us talked of taking a trip somewhere together, but that never materialized.

I could tell of many good times with others from the *Liscome Bay* as well as friends from Jim's ship the *Alpine*. The Votes, Lambs, Weisses, and Andrews became lifelong friends who have added to our many memories made possible by the days Jim spent in the Navy.

As a result of Jim's love of story-telling we had several amusing things happen through the passing years. The basic story remained the same but he liked to embellish or emphasize a point for a specific audience. I will relate a few incidents.

A friend who was a retired Naval officer always requested Jim retell the experience he had with the Admiral when Jim said he wanted the Admiral's job!

When Jim was principal of a high school he taught a history class to keep in touch with the students. Frequently some student side-tracked the planned lesson by asking a question about Mr. Beasley's military service. The class thought it was great fun to lead Jim astray of the day's lesson plan—they had really pulled a smart trick! What they did not realize Jim had set the stage for two reasons. One: They were about the age Jim was when he enlisted so he liked to talk to that age group. And two: He knew real live stories created more interest in history than mere pages in a book.

Epilogue

On one occasion when he was telling a psychologist the stories about the strange dreams his friends had before the tragic sinking of his ship, he injected a phrase about spirits, and was told he should go to someone to analyze his thoughts. His response was "I don't want someone messing with my brain—there is no telling what they might discover!"

To sum up Jim's experiences in the Navy, I'll use his words: "My days in the United States Navy were some of the best days of my life and also some of the worst. I learned at the age of eighteen that man can change God's creation from beautiful to ugly in a very short time."

Bibliography

Mooney, James L., ed. *Dictionary of American Fighting Ships*, Vol. 1. Washington, D.C.: Naval Historical Center, Department of the Navy, 1991.

Morison, Samuel Eliot. *History of United States Naval Operations in World War II.* 15 vols. Boston: Little, Brown, 1947–1962.

Noles, James L., Jr. *Twenty-Three Minutes to Eternity: The Final Voyage of the Escort Carrier USS Liscome Bay.* Tuscaloosa: University of Alabama Press, 2010.

Potter, Elmer B., and Chester W. Nimitz. *Sea Power: A Naval History.* Englewood Cliffs, NJ: Prentice-Hall, 1960.

Reader's Digest Illustrated Story of World War II. New York: Random House, 1969.

USS Alpine Yearbook, 1945.

Youngblood, William T. *The Little Giants: U.S. Escort Carriers Against Japan.* Annapolis: Naval Institute Press, 1987.

Index

Numbers in *bold italics* indicate pages with illustrations

Adams, Albert 130
Admiral Nimitz Museum 132
Admiralty Islands 77, 83
Alabama 66–68
Alameda Naval Air Station 21, 63
Alcatraz 21
Aleutian Islands 28, 90
Allee, Dorothy 148, 155
Allee, Phalan *128*, *130*, *138*, 140, *142*, 148
Allies 106
USS *Alpine* 71, *72*, *73*, 74–86, 88, 89, 91, 93–96, 98–100, 103–105, 108, 109, 111–113, 127
Alpine Yearbook 146, 147
Amphibious Force 105
Andrews, Hilda *125*, 126, 153
Andrews, Wally 54, 55, 64, 65, 100, *125*, 126
Army 81, 84, 86, 87
Asia 29
Astoria, Oregon 17, *18*, 20
atomic bomb 104, 106–108
Avengers *22*

Bailor *107*
Banner Elk, North Carolina *125*
Beasley, Clarence 3, 4, 13, 117
Beasley, James Arthur 3
Beasley, James Claude (Sam) 3, *4*, *6*, *8*, *12*, *16*, *17*, *27*, 64, *89*, *95*, *98*, *110*, *118*, *122*, *124*, *128*, *130*, *134*, *137*, *140*, *142*, *149*, 152, 155
Beasley, John *7*, 8
Beasley, Lowe Beasley *118*, *125*, *140*, *149*
Beasley, Paul 4, 13, 117
Beasley, Ruby 7
Beaumont, Sam *142*
Benson, Charles *130*
Beymer, John *142*
Biak 79
Blankenship, Joe *142*
Bohn, Dorothy 154, 155
Bohn, Leonard *128*, 129, *130*, 131, 132, 136, *138*, *142*
Bougainville 90
Branson, Missouri 139
The *Branson Belle* *140*
Breeden, Charles *130*

Bremerton, Washington 17, 20
Brown, Paul 15
Buckner Bay 105
Bush, Lester *130*

California 61, 63
Camp Cladstrop 18
Carley, Lt. Robert 50, 145
Catawba College 117, 119, 154
Chapman *89*
Charleston, South Carolina 127, *128*, *134*
Chicago, Illinois 12
China 29, 91, 105, 109
Churchill, Winston 29
Clark Field 84
Click *89*
Coast Guard 81
Coeur d'Alenc 16
Columbia River 18, 20, 72
Coronado 138
Corpus Christi 132
Cozard *89*
Crommelin, Captain John 51
Cruse, Donald *142*

Des Moines, Iowa 132
Doe, Pete *110*, *122*
Doolittle, Jimmie 91
Duff, Signalman 54, 55

Elon College 9
Emerald Isle, North Carolina 121, 148, 152, 153
Eniwetok 74, 76, 90, 103
Enola Gay 106
Europe 29

Farragut, Idaho 14–17
Ferebee, Maj. Tom 106, 107
Ferguson, Edward 142
Fifth Fleet 95
Fisher, Bill *134*, *142*
Ford Island 26
Forrest *89*
Franklin High School 9
Fredericksburg, Texas 131

159

Index

Freeman, Roger *130*, *142*
Freeman, Vera 155

Germany 28
Gilbert Islands 28, 29, 31, 32
Golden Gate Bridge 21
Goss, Signalman Gerald 54, 55, *77*, *89*, *98*, 135
Great Lakes Naval Training Station *12*, 13, 15, 66
Griffith, Andy 9
Guadalcanal 89
Guam 29, 73-77, 80, 90

Hall, Commander Finley E. *19*, 50, 127
Hannibal, Missouri 131, 140, 141
Halsey[apost]s Third Fleet 79
Harris, Kenneth J. *128*, *130*, 131-133, *142*
Hawaii 23, 26-29, 48, 51, 52, 56, 57, 59, 73, 76, 97, 103, 112
Heater, Gabriel 28
Hellcats 22
Henslee, Bill *110*, 125
Hickman Fields 26
Hirohito, Emperor 108
Hiroshima 107
Hitler, Adolf 29, 98
Hollandia, New Guinea 79
Honold, James *128*
Honolulu, Hawaii 56
Honor Flight *150*, 151, 152
USS *Hope* *99*, 100, 126
USS *Hornet* 91
USS *Hughes* 45, 47, 48, 51, 52, *53*, 59
Hunt, Lt. Glenn 41

Independence, Missouri 133
Italy 29
Iwo Jima 91

Japan 28, 29, 34, 81, 90-92, 96, 100, 104-107
Japanese Zeroes 27
Jinsen 105
Johnson *85*, *89*, *107*
Jonas, Edward *142*
Jones, Irvin *130*

Kaiser Shipyard 18
kamakazi 78, 79, 81, 83-85
Kehl, Tony *128*, *130*
King Neptune 30
Kinston, North Carolina 122
Korea 105
Koupe *107*
Krantz, Jack 132
Kwajalein 90

Lamb, Gladys *123*
Lamb, John 122, *123*

Lawson, Maggie 3
Lawson, Martha (grandmother) 6, 54
LeMay, Maj. Gen. Curtis 104
Lennon, Joseph *128*
Lewis and Clark 18
USS *Lexington* 89, 132, 134
Leyte 76-81, 83
Leyte Gulf 79
Lingayen Gulf 84-86
LisBay Totem Pole 146
USS *Liscome Bay* 17, *18*, *19*, 20, 21, *22*, 23, 26-29, 30, 32-34, 38-43, 47-51, 52, 53, 56-59, 61, *62*, 63, 65, 68, 70-72, 74, 76, 81-83, 86, 126, 127, 131, 134, 141, 142, 144, 145, 147, 154
Liscome Bay Association 128, 130, 132, *136*, 138, *139*, 141, *142*, 153
Lombardo Guy 101
Luzani, Chief Signalman Lloyd 41
Luzon 84, 86

MacArthur, Gen. Douglas 29, 79, 89, 99
Makin Island 31-34, 48, 50, 51, 59, 76, 90
Manila Bay 84
Manus Island 79, 83
Mariana Islands 73, 74, 90
Marines 81, 87
Mark Twain Showboat 140
Marshall Islands 29, 90, 103
McFedries, George *142*
USS *Midway* 89, 141
Miller, Dorie 144
Miller, Glenn 101
Millersburg 124
USS *Missouri* 108
USS *Morris* 50
Morrison, Samuel Eliot 145
Mount Airy, North Carolina 8, 10, 12, 68, 69, 115, 117
Mt. Soledad 141
Mt. Suribachi 91
Moyer *89*
Mullinnix, Radm. Henry M. 22, 50, 145-147
Murphy, Bob 125
Murphy, Jim *89*, *98*, 124
Murrow, Edward R. 28
Museum of Naval Aviation 139

Nagasaki 107
Nagoya 111
Nashville, Tennessee 119, 120
Navy 81, 153-156
Navy Reserve 119, 120
New Guinea 77, 79, 83, 84
New Orleans, Louisiana 67
Newland, North Carolina 120, 148
Nimitz, Adm. Chester 29, 90
Norfolk, Virginia 112, 115

160

Index

USS *North Carolina* 104
North Carolina State College 117

Oahu 26
Oakland, California 103
Okinawa 88, 91, 93, 95, 99, 100, 104
"Oympia" 108
180th meridian 30, 31, *73*, 74

Pacific Fleet 53
Pacific Ocean 20, 28, 81, 97, 98
Panama Canal 112
Parsons, Capt. William 106
Peabody College 119
Pearl Harbor 9, 23, 27, 28, 48, 49, 53, 72, 73, 76, 97, 103
Pensacola, Florida 138, 139
Philippine Islands 29, 76, 77, 81, 84, 88, 89, 91, 93, 99, 105
Pinder, Willard *130*, *142*
Point Loma 21, 138
Polson *89*
Portland, Oregon 66, 69, 71
Price, Robert 137
Puget Sound 17, 20
Purple Heart 74, 147

Quartermaster Corps 86

Raleigh, North Carolina 11, 68, 117
Red Cross 56, 57
Reilly, Lt. Cdr. George K. 71, 112
Roosevelt, Pres. Franklin D. 29, 96
Roosevelt, James (2nd Raider Battalion) 50
Rowe, Lt. Cdr. John 50
Ryukyu Islands 88, 91, 93

Saipan 29, 90, 97
Salina, Kansas 127, 129
Salisbury 117
San Diego, California 21, 23, 26, 72, 73, 105, 109, *136*, *137*, 138, 141, 142
San Francisco, California 21, 61, 99
San Pedro Naval Base 22
USS *Saratoga* 61, *62*, 63
Schmitt, Edward *142*
Schouten Islands 79
Seaport Village, California 141
Seattle, Washington 17, 20, 97, 98, 100, 101
Seventh Fleet 84
shipmates *82*
Smith, Lt. Gardner 40
Smith, Steward 52, 56
Solomon Islands 89, 90
Spruance, Adm. Raymond 29, 90
Star of India 138
Stokes County, North Carolina 3

Stoner, Albert 127, *128*, 129, 131
Subic Bay 86

Tabata, Lt. Commodore 146
Table Rock Lake 140
Tacoma, Washington 111, 112
Taku 105
Tarawa 35, 90
Thirty-eighth Infantry 86
Tibbits, Col. Paul 106
Tijuana 110, 141
Tinian 90, 106
Tokyo Rose 53
Trevino, Teofilo *128*, *130*
Truman, Pres. Harry S. 96, 104, 106–108, 133
Tsingtaot 105
typhoon 97

Ulithi 104, 105
Unbehagen, Pete 23, 33, 54, 55, 68, *98*, 101, 153
United Nations 99
United States 53, 97–99, 106
USO 58, 69, 98, 100, 101

V-E Day 98
Vancouver, Washington 18
Veterans Day 152
von Kempf, Paul *130*, *135*, *142*
Vote, Dottie 123, *124*
Vote, Norman *89*, *98*, 123, *124*, 153

Wake Island 29
Walz, Don 129, *130*
Washington, D.C. 150, 152
Watsabrugh *89*
Weihaiwei 105
Weiss, Harry *89*, *110*, 121, *122*
Welk, Lawrence 101
Western Caroline Islands 104
Wiesler, Jim *133*
Wiesler, Mary Jane Hall *133*
Wildcats *22*, 23, 30, 32, 36, 37
Wilker, Dale 88, 90, 91, 127, 129, *137*
Williams, Chester R. (Chuck) 36, 55, 66–68, *89*
Wiltsie, Capt. Irving D. *19*, 145, 147
Winston-Salem, North Carolina 68
Woodham, Helen 154
Woodham, Tim *130*, *137*, *138*, 139, *142*
World Security Charter 98
World War II Memorial 150
World War II Victory Medal 147

Yadkin County, North Carolina 119
USS *Yorktown* 37, 127–129, *134*, 136
Youtz, Willard *142*

"Zekes" 85

www.ingramcontent.com/pod-product-compliance
Ingram Content Group UK Ltd.
Pitfield, Milton Keynes, MK11 3LW, UK
UKHW042016140426
5217IPUK00015B/1209